ALSO BY LAURIE LISLE

Portrait of an Artist:
A Biography of Georgia O'Keeffe

Louise Nevelson: A Passionate Life

Without Child:
Challenging the Stigma of Childlessness

FOUR
TENTHS
of an
ACRE

RANDOM HOUSE
NEW YORK

FOUR
TENTHS
of an
ACRE

Reflections on
a Gardening Life

LAURIE LISLE

Published in the United States by Random House,
an imprint of The Random House Publishing Group,
a division of Random House, Inc., New York.

Random House and colophon are registered trademarks
of Random House, Inc.

LIBRARY OF CONGRESS CATALOGING-IN-PUBLICATION DATA
Lisle, Laurie.
Four tenths of an acre: reflections on a gardening life / Laurie Lisle.
p.   cm.
ISBN 1-4000-6167-9
1. Lisle, Laurie. 2. Gardeners—Sharon (Conn.: Town)—Biography.
3. Journalists—Sharon (Conn.: Town)—Biography. 4. Gardening—
Sharon (Conn.: Town)—Biography. I. Title.
SB63.L53A3 2005
635'.092—dc22
[B]   2004051494

Random House website address: www.atrandom.com

Printed in the United States of America on acid-free paper

2 4 6 8 9 7 5 3 1

First Edition

Book design by Susan Turner

To my mother, Adeline Cole Congdon,

who gave me the gift of gardening

In view of the vital part played
by the green leaf in the state known as life,
there is no subject more worthy of study.

STANLEY B. WHITEHEAD,
Encyclopedia of Gardening

preface

When I moved from the city to the country, I had no idea how to turn the strip of grass behind my house on a New England village green into the gorgeous flower garden in my mind's eye. Nevertheless, I wanted to do it myself. I learned as I went along from my mother and friends as well as from my reading, together with my own observations and experiences in the backyard.

My garden-in-progress was always on my mind, so I wanted to write about "some lost paradise, a part of nature," as I noted in a journal a few years ago. I eventually decided to write about the decade of my forties through the "green glasses" of a gardener. My garden notebook grew into this modern pastoral, part garden book and part memoir, which celebrates the role of nature in a contemporary life. It is also about love and loss, work and play, roots and restlessness, intimacy and independence, refuge and risk, solitude and sociability. It is about the struggle between sunlight and shadow, in all senses of the words.

Once, when flying into an airport in spring over the soft, rolling hills of northwestern Connecticut, I remembered a dream about gazing down on an appealing and intriguing green landscape that was mine to explore. I felt very glad to live in the country, where it was green at least half the year.

The natural world sustains the manufactured one with increasing difficulty, so I hope this book is a reminder of the importance of that emblem of nature called a garden.

contents

FOUR
TENTHS
of an
ACRE

one

ARRIVAL

——◆►◄ ►◄◆——

This surprising wild joy
was with me all yesterday,
and it continues—a little
less intense—today. . . .
The high summer beauty—
fields of wildflowers,
the river, the dramatic hills
and fields. Even the sky—
sharp-edged clouds now
like western ones.

August 21, 1984

IT WAS ON THE LAST DAY OF March when I drove up an icy hill, turned onto the main street of a Connecticut village, and parked in front of a clapboard house. I got out of the car and gave my new home a searching look. Its narrow facade had four tall windows and a doorway sheltered by a little roof, while all the ells, entrances, porches, and balconies, glittering under a layer of fresh snow, hinted at a long and enigmatic past. The day before, at my rented house on eastern Long Island, a blustery rainstorm had postponed moving day. Here, a hundred miles north of the coast, the storm had left a surface of light over the land.

At least a foot of snow covered the short walkway from the sidewalk to the nearest doorway. I had not thought to bring a shovel and, in fact, did not even own one. Crossing Main Street, I walked up a slope toward a hardware store, crunching through the brittle white crust covering delicate crystals that coated the village green. I trudged up the steps of the old store and went inside. The unpainted wooden floor creaked loudly as I walked over to a stack of bright red snow shovels. An elderly man at the cash register smiled sympathetically; it had been a long winter.

Leaving the store with the shovel, I could see from my elevated vantage point on Upper Main Street many of the old colonial houses lining the green, most of them typically painted white with black shutters. My little house below looked nicely nestled in. It was so close to the sidewalk that during future snowstorms I was certain I could get mail, groceries, newspapers, books, money, or whatever else I needed on foot. By settling on a street in this small town called Sharon, I felt, above all, a sense of relief. I had been there only two or three times before, but it felt familiar, like home, because I had grown up in New England.

The red aluminum shovel had a flat, light blade, and as I shoveled the walk, the melting snow slid off easily. When I finished and went inside, sunlight was pouring through large glass panes into the empty rooms. As I walked from room to room, the moving van arrived. In came the couch with the pale cotton upholstery that my former husband and I had bought at Bloomingdale's for our Manhattan apartment a decade earlier. Then the movers carried in the replica of an eighteenth-century corner cupboard, which my father had finished making the year I was born, and put it in the dining room. This mute mahogany personage—the height of a tall man—had always been a paternal presence that stood watch over me in childhood, even though more often than not it reminded me of my father's absence. It was because of his recent death, as well as my divorce, that I was able to make a down payment on this property. It would be good alchemy, I thought, to try to turn sadness and deep disappointment into something different in this new place.

Chests, chairs, and other family furniture appeared, the pieces I felt I had no right to own so soon. They were mine because of earlier upheaval in the family—my mother's divorce from my father, and then his divorce from his next wife, who had unexpectedly named me the beneficiary in her will. When I was in college she had died suddenly, so as a very young woman I became the uneasy owner of the old Vermont house where she and my father once lived. Before that house was sold, I had saved some of its chests and chairs and even an old iron frying pan that were now with me in Connecticut. After the movers finally closed up their truck and drove away, I had a pleasant sensation of possession. As I began to unpack books and dishes and hang clothes in closets, I realized that it was now up to me to pull together fragments of broken lives into something new, and whole, and entirely my own. I had recently passed the age of forty, and I was aware of time passing.

For months I had been in a fever to find a house. It was an instinct to compensate for the collapse of my previous life, even though it was a life I no longer wanted. Those months had felt ripe with potential but a little frightening, too. Still, I might have remained in limbo a little longer except that I had a book to write. I had always liked inland hills, so one autumn day I had driven around Litchfield County in northwestern Connecticut with notebook and pen beside me. That day I drove right through Sharon to the next town of Salisbury, where I parked in front of a real estate office. I met with a realtor about my age and told her what I wanted: a village house with a wonderful room for writing and an apartment to rent out between books. When I returned a few weeks later to look at listings, it began to snow heavily, and the realtor invited me to stay overnight at her house on Sharon Mountain instead of trying to drive back to New York. After the power went out, the night was very dark and cold, and I was glad when the dawn broke clear. I drove down the mountainside amid unfolding views of snowy fields bounded by dark rows of trees and stone walls, more certain than ever that I wanted a house in a village.

It was on that wintry day when I first saw my house. The real estate agent told me about the soundness of the structure and pointed out the attractive architectural details, but what was most alluring to me was the way daylight flooded the old rooms. I also liked the little fireplace, the bedroom with balconies, the bright room I had chosen for writing, the pleasing arrangement of the rooms. Wildly excited, I made a low offer that was turned down and immediately made another, a little higher. As the negotiations dragged on, I was so nervous that I would lie motionless on my bed in the middle of the day, praying that the house would really become mine. Finally, when my bid was accepted a few days later, I was so elated that I began scribbling down a rush of decorating ideas.

The truth is that finding a house was much more important than having a garden, at least at first. I was, in fact, staking everything on the possession of this place, a house of my own, an ordinary collection of walls, doorways, and windows, which I hoped I would never have to leave or ever want to leave, either. Right after the movers drove away, I walked to the back of the house and looked out a window at the yard, which I had never seen without a camouflage of snow. All I could see was a length of cleared land with trees and buildings around it, an empty expanse of shining snow sloping slightly away to the west. It looked large to me, and while I worried if I would be able to take care of it, I also liked the idea of having a garden. I had already done a rough drawing of flower beds, patios, paths, and trees; it was an ambitious plan based on very little experience or knowledge. That March day there were only leafless bushes and trees in the backyard, just sharp sticks silhouetted against the starkness; without leaves on their branches, I could not identify any of them. I noticed that the top branches of a tree near the house almost touched the high roof, and that shrubs and saplings grew haphazardly in no evident pattern.

A neighbor's white picket fence stuck out of the snow on one side of the yard, and on the other side stood my barn, where snow was dripping off the roof and making bright puddles below. As I looked toward the far end of the property, I became more worried. When I had seen the surveyor's map of my less than half acre a few weeks earlier, I was shocked at how very long and narrow a rectangle it actually was; on paper, as if seen from above, it looked to me like a fairway on a golf course, and I wondered how I could turn such an awful shape into a graceful garden. I also stared with despair at a chain-link fence glinting harshly in the sunlight and severing the backyard; the realtor had told me that a previous owner of the house had dogs. Beyond the barn and barely visible from the window, a tangle of bare branches towered over one long side of the land.

Within a week the air got warmer, and the dissolving snow revealed a square concrete platform behind the house that looked like the foundation of a former kennel. Farther back the melting snow had left a long, jagged line down the middle of the yard, as if it were in the throes of a powerful tide; on the side saturated by sun, the ground was greenish brown, and in the partial shade, it stayed grayish white. As the whiteness retreated during the next few days, it left behind only soggy leaves and struggling sod, all littered with sticks and broken branches. It looked like no one had ever gardened there before, but I was determined to imagine my unprepossessing property as a garden. I knew enough about growing to watch where shadows fell and where sunlight lingered, as the sun moved from the front to the back of the yard during the day.

One sunny weekend in April the grass suddenly looked greener, and I realized with a pang of anxiety that I did not own a lawn mower. Meanwhile, masses of rampant weeds— jewelweed, bedstraw, nightshade, lady's thumb, and stinging nettle—shot up behind bushes and along the edges of the yard. Alarmed at the realization that I must uproot the weeds before they set seed, I pulled weed after weed during the following weeks in a frantic race with nature.

As it got greener outside, I was busy inside. Only days after moving in, the basement had filled with several inches of water during a heavy rainstorm. The plumber, while pumping out the groundwater, noticed an empty sump pump pit, and then he pointed out that the furnace was on cement blocks and the cellar was full of raised wooden pallets, making me realize that a flooded basement was not an unexpected occurrence. (Years later, after many more floods, I learned that there was an old streambed under the green across the street from the house.) Almost immediately after settling into my house, I had bought a cocker spaniel puppy from a breeder on Long Island, and began to house-train her. On another rainy day, as I carried the puppy down the cellar stairs to put her out in the yard,

I saw water sloshing around in the basement again. That after-noon, as the puppy kept wetting the floor upstairs and the rain-water kept rising downstairs, I sobbed in frustration before pulling myself back together again. A few weeks later, after I had painted the ugly concrete platform green, the puppy man-aged to roll in the only spot that was not entirely dry. Over-whelmed by the weeds and the water and the puppy, I struggled to keep my mind on writing.

Outside, as the days grew longer, buds on branches began to uncurl into leaves. I recognized many of the bushes and trees behind the house; I pulled their names from my memory of my mother's and grandmothers' gardens and looked up oth-ers in books in the small stone library across the green. Maple leaves opened on the tall tree near the house. Six or so shrubs alongside the chain-link fence put out lilac leaflets; leaves of others revealed themselves as roses of Sharon, which, not sur-prisingly, were planted in abundance in town. At the back of the yard near a neighbor's white clapboard garage, a row of scraggly bushes turned out to be privet. I also found a large oval bed of overgrown irises planted gracelessly in the middle of the grass.

As I tried to identify more of the new growth, a woman I met in the hardware store told me about Fred McGourty, a well-respected horticulturist who, along with his wife, Mary Ann, owned a garden and nursery of unusual perennials in the nearby town of Norfolk. I telephoned, and Fred, a short, square, middle-aged man, whose center of gravity seemed close to the earth, came over for an hour. At first he stood with his legs firmly planted on the ground and looked around, tactfully saying nothing about the strange dimensions of my yard. Then, as I followed him around with my tape recorder, he identified the rest of the plantings for me, all of whose common and Latin names were on the tip of his tongue.

The news, delivered gravely, was not good. He told me in his authoritative baritone that the tree behind the house was a young Norway maple that would rapidly grow to three times its present size. The problem, he explained, was that it would be difficult to plant anything under it because of its dense shade and shallow roots. He named a lovely little tree with smooth gray bark and pointed pale leaves a silver maple, but he warned me that it was a messy, weak specimen that would also grow very fast. Along the edges of the grassy area he noted thinning pines and languishing white ashes. Worst of all, he stated glumly, rainwater falling off the overhanging barn roof would make it impossible to grow flowers in the sun alongside the barn, exactly where I envisioned a lush border. It was where my mind's eye imagined the gorgeous flower garden that followed old-fashioned horticultural rules, where low blossoms graduate to higher ones, rounded masses contrast with vertical spikes, and something is always in bloom.

Plant shrubs like azaleas and rhododendrons next to the barn instead of flowers, Fred told me sensibly. Dig up the lone rosebush here and the struggling rhododendron there or else move them into groupings. Move the daylilies from under the maple. If I did not have an aversion to pachysandra, plant it along the north side of the house, he advised. Get rid of the poorly placed iris bed because it interrupted the view to the end of the yard. Take advantage of the surprising depth of the property, he went on in an amiable way, by planting at the back a grove of white birch trees against dark evergreens like yews or arborvitaes, and then link them together with ferns and groundcovers. An excellent idea, I thought, but also an expensive one.

Then Fred paused, as if momentarily uncertain of what he was saying, and asked me a question. Did I want plantings along the edges of my long rectangle to take the shape of an hourglass or a reverse hourglass? I hesitated and was unable to answer. I did not know. I was also well aware that, if asked, he would gladly plan and plant the garden for me, but I instinctively resisted. I could not imagine anyone designing my garden-to-be, any more than I could imagine anyone ghost-writing my book. And, besides, trial and error would make it mine, no matter how long it took.

BEFORE MY ARRIVAL IN SHARON I HAD LEFT PLACES FOR a number of reasons, once after a love affair and another time at the end of a marriage. When I was in my twenties I was eager to explore what was outside myself, as if it would tell me more about what was inside. After college I worked for a newspaper in my hometown of Providence, but I increasingly felt the pull of New York. A boyfriend had taken me to Chumley's, a tiny hangout in Greenwich Village without its name on the door, where men and women talked intensely in a haze of cigarette smoke. In my black mohair sweater and pleated white chiffon skirt, I didn't exactly blend in with the Village bohemians, but the passionate seriousness of the atmosphere appealed to me, and I wanted more of it. Back in Rhode Island, when I told an uncle that I was leaving for New York, he shook his head gravely and predicted that nothing good would come of it. He had drawn up a family genealogy going all the way back to the seventeenth century, and he knew that most of my mother's side of the family had never strayed far from New England. I'm sure he thought it was where I should stay, too.

The September I turned twenty-five, I packed a suitcase and left the graceful steeples, small parks, and steep streets— the prettiness of Providence—and headed for Manhattan with a stony determination to stay. I rented a room in the Pickwick Arms, a midtown residential hotel near my new job at a magazine. I liked unpacking in the minuscule bedroom and did not even mind the element of danger in sharing an adjoining bathroom with a stranger. What I remember vividly about those autumn weeks were the tiny East Side florist shops full of exquisite and exotic blossoms that were barely visible through foggy window glass. From time to time I used to step inside one or another of these shops for a few minutes just to inhale the moist, fragrant, pungent smell of perpetual spring.

A few months later I gladly left the hotel for an apartment in the West Village. It was on the ground floor of a brownstone with a shadowy little garden in back, a small area of square flagstones edged with beds of battered dark green ivy. One Saturday morning in early spring, when the weak sunlight was warming the flagstones and making the soil give off a sweet, earthy aroma, I got to work. I gathered some kitchen knives, forks, spoons, and scissors along with a garbage bag, and pushed open the heavy door to the garden. I picked up the newspapers, paper cups, and other trash that had blown into it over the winter, swept the stones, clipped off broken and browned ivy leaves, and raked the dirt around the plants, which were struggling to put forth new growth. After the owners returned on Sunday evening and looked down from their back windows, they asked me if a professional gardener had rejuvenated their garden. I was pleased because it was my first inkling that I had an instinct for that kind of thing.

My life in New York was almost all that I wanted it to be. Everywhere was the intensity I had sensed at Chumley's—at meetings of the Village Independent Democrats down the street and during demonstrations of the Women's Liberation Movement. Around that time I was impressed by the large retrospective of the paintings of Georgia O'Keeffe at the Whitney Museum of American Art. The serene, pellucid renderings of endless sky made me feel something about clarity and freedom, and, above all, about the possibility of spending more time outside the city.

There were disappointments, too, like losing the garden apartment. But in Manhattan it was easy to begin all over again, at least for a while. I found another brownstone apartment on the Upper West Side with what could be called, with a stretch of the imagination, a garden. It was completely paved with concrete and almost always shaded by tall apartment buildings around it. Shafts of light arrived at odd times of day, more dependent on the shapes of the surrounding structures than on the position of the sun in the sky. Nonetheless, I began to pot plants and put them outside, including three small gardenias. When I returned from work in the early evenings, I would rinse the soot off their dark, glossy leaves and soak their soil. When delicate root tips emerged from holes in the bottoms of the pots, I would move them to bigger ones. Gradually the gardenias grew into bushes that put forth profusions of outrageously fragrant white flowers. When I touched my nose to a velvety petal, its ambrosia would remind me of Easter Sundays in childhood or wrist corsages at teenage dances, and would arouse fantasies about more indulgent ways of being.

After a few years in New York, I began to live a double life, at least in my mind. I had taken a vacation in New Mexico, and I began to long for days drenched in brilliant sunlight, more time to write and be with friends, and the presence of an overarching western sky. Yet I hesitated to make the move, wondering whether without the intensity of the city I would lose my edge, or whatever it was that made me want to write. Then there was my relationship with the man I eventually married, which, if not exactly happy, was at least steady. Instead, I left my job to write a biography of O'Keeffe, an artist whose passion was the beauty of the natural world. I gave up the second garden apartment for one on the twelfth floor of a building on nearby West End Avenue with my husband-to-be, where the magnificent gardenias immediately withered and died in the dry indoor air.

I worked in the apartment's tiny maid's room, a space I painted entirely white—walls, ceiling, floor, bookcases, even filing cabinet—in an attempt to make it feel larger. I tried to screen out the sight of the security gate and fire escape at the window with a white floor-to-ceiling pole holding scraggly green-and-white-striped spider plants, whose hanging, sprouting tendrils formed a big tangled mass. For sky I hung posters of O'Keeffe's peaceful pale blue-and-white cloud paintings high on a wall. There was nothing I could do, however, about the screeches of subways and sirens that continually pierced the glass and brick walls of the building.

During this time I had an emerging, almost primal longing for vegetation, for weather, and for seasons. When spring arrived in the city, it was barely perceptible except as a gust of warm air, or more light in the evenings, or the sight of pale green fringe on a fenced-in sapling along the sidewalk. More and more often I would pause to look at a lovingly tended neighborhood garden behind iron bars. Or I would notice a flowering pink or red azalea in front of a brownstone attached to a metal railing with a locked bicycle chain. On a weekend away from the city, I found myself falling to my knees onto an ordinary little plot of grass outside a motel, as if it were the Garden of Eden.

One afternoon in Manhattan when I was aching for greenness, I took a book to a bench amid the uncut grass and neglected trees in Central Park. Looking up I saw three boys stealthily approaching me, so I slammed the book shut, jumped up, and walked quickly away. After that day I rarely read or lingered alone in the park. Around that time I realized that it wasn't information or stimulation that I wanted anymore, but a kind of inwardness, and the city gradually lost its grip on me. It was the spring when I spotted an early copy of my biography of O'Keeffe in the window of a Madison Avenue bookstore that, hoping I could earn a living outside the city, I was finally ready to go.

My marriage was unhappy, and in September on the eve of my thirty-ninth birthday, I got into my car and headed for Sag Harbor on the eastern end of Long Island to sign a lease for a winter rental in another writer's house. As I drove away from the illuminated city, I was gripped by terror at what I was doing—leaving my husband—and it would not have surprised me if the darkening sky had fallen on my head. As I pushed eastward, I became aware that I was driving toward a large, low harvest moon that was drenching the distant, rippling surface of the sea in white light. It felt as if the moon were pulling me forward with its magnetic force.

During the winter on the East End, I felt soothed by the

string of old villages, set among flat fields under a wide sky and awash in luminous light reflected off the ocean. I did things I had never done before, like allowing an amateur pilot to take me up in a single-engine airplane. Despite the danger, the exciting flights gave me a different and fascinating perspective on the meandering chalky coastline, the pattern of ponds on the wintry land, and the placement of islands in the bay far below. When I felt melancholy, I liked to follow a path through a thick tangle of seaside brush full of tame chickadees until it abruptly opened onto a wide beach. I would walk on the sand to a hillock with a tiny pond encircled by beach grasses and sea roses, and then turn around and go back along the water and through the thicket, contented once again.

One February afternoon inside my rented house, I suddenly noticed that the light outside had lost its winter dullness. I was passing through a room with dark rose walls when everything seemed charged with a glorious difference. As long as the feeling lasted, it felt like being bathed in a benevolent glow. It was as if patterns in my brain had abruptly rearranged themselves, the way colored pieces of glass do in a kaleidoscope. I wanted the moment to last, but after a minute or so it dissolved like a dream. Its memory remained, however, reminding me of the ever-present possibility of rapture. It was also the signal of the inexorable change that had happened over the winter, and I knew that I was not going to move back to New York.

THAT FIRST SPRING IN SHARON THE SWORDLIKE LEAVES of the irises in the middle of the yard began to lengthen, and then green-sheathed buds appeared. One evening after returning home, I looked out a back window and saw in the twilight that the thick clump of irises had blotches of color held aloft like little flags. Realizing that the buds had begun to burst open, I rushed outside with the puppy at my heels. What I found was an extravagance of fluted blossoms as big as my open hand. Three ruffled petals stood upright and another three dangled down. Each flower was deep purple and white, with caterpillar-like shapes inside, and a slight perfume that took my breath away. They looked so blatant and bold: they flaunted their beauty, defiantly exposing their delicate tissues and unopened buds to the elements. That evening the blossoming of the iris felt like such a lavish gift of nature, and one given so generously, that it marked my capitulation to the gardening life.

When I returned inside, I looked under *I* in a gardening encyclopedia my mother had given me to learn more about my bearded irises. Over the next few days other colors appeared. Beige blossoms unfurled to display fuzzy orange growths, or "beards," as did burgundy ones with dusky brown beards, and deep blue blooms with even darker, almost black beards. Some of the straight stalks became so weighted down with flowers

that I had to tie them to stakes so they would not fall over, especially in the rain. Papery-thin petals were perfect for a day or two, and then they would suddenly shrivel, as if their source of sap had dried up. Over the next few weeks I floated iris blossoms in shallow bowls and cut stems of blossoms to arrange in tall vases. Finally, when they all were spent and there were no more buds to open, I clipped the stalks to the ground, leaving only stiff green leaves standing for the rest of the season.

In the village library I read that archaeologists discovered carved images of irises in the ruins of Egyptian temples and painted likenesses on the walls of ancient Greek palaces. In Greece, purple irises were traditionally placed on women's graves because the goddess Iris, the deity of the rainbow, was believed to lead their souls to paradise. Irises in vases and in gardens are pictured on old Japanese silk scrolls. The iris is also seen on Italian altarpieces as early as the thirteenth century. In France, the flower was stylized as the fleur-de-lis and emblazoned on the flags and crowns of royalty for centuries. Besides its symbolic uses, the iris had practical applications over the years: its rhizome, or tuberous root, was used to make medicines, perfumes, liquors, and other precious liquids.

Working on a new edition of the O'Keeffe biography during my first summer in Sharon, I realized with a start that the artist had been exactly my age, forty-one, when she had made the momentous visit to New Mexico that had changed her life. As I leafed through a garden catalog that offered irises, I remembered one of her paintings from 1926, *Black Iris,* that is usually on view at the Metropolitan Museum of Art in New York. It is an enormous close-up, a butterfly's-eye view, of an iris with purplish upper petals and blackish bottom ones. I realized that the dark iris in the painting wasn't really black at all, at least not inky black like the newer cultivars in the catalog. I remembered that she was unable to find the rare so-called black iris except in New York florist shops for a few weeks in the spring. It became apparent that the array of colorful irises in my yard was an inadvertent gift from a stranger who had once owned the property, someone who may have ordered the "rainbow collection" from an earlier version of the very catalog I was looking at. Whatever the case, I was the inheritor of a tradition that had begun thousands of years ago and was continuing in my backyard today.

The following spring I labeled the irises by color, and after they finished blooming I took Fred McGourty's advice and dug them up and planted them elsewhere. I grouped the purples and whites together as well as the other colors. As he had predicted, my narrow piece of land looked better than before. Around that time my mother gave me irises from her garden that eventually put forth exquisite white petals with bright yellow beards. Put outside a window with a low sill, when they opened on the other side of the glass, they were like an opulent floral wave from her. One May I noted in my gardening notebook: *"White—huge—iris in front are blooming—dramatic— gorgeous."*

The irises would test my devotion when they became

infested with borers, disgusting pinkish worms that eat away at rhizomes. I spent an anguished afternoon digging up the plants, pulling off rotting leaves, destroying the borers, discarding eviscerated rhizomes, and replanting the remains in a raised bed behind the barn, in the hope that they would tolerate hot afternoon sun and dryness under the overhang of the roof. Eventually I became resigned to the loss, remembering that Fred had advised me against having too many irises in a border because they bloom so briefly. As the survivors gradually formed thick clumps and then put forth fewer flowers, I divided them repeatedly and gave many away, so now they burst open every June in a number of gardens in Sharon.

I wondered why, like an earthling, I enjoyed inland hills more than the seashore, and why one person is drawn to earth and another to water. Although I spent summers by the shore, I never cared for the hot light of the beach in Rhode Island. At camp in Maine I loved wrapping fragrant green ferns around my waist, as filtered sunlight transformed the pinewoods into an enchanted forest. When I went to boarding school near Sharon, I rhapsodized in my diary the October of my senior year about the month's magnificence, as green leaves turned into "unbelievable orangey reds and stark yellows." The flamboyance of the foliage must have been followed by a snowy winter and an early spring, because the yearbook editors noted that my favorite expression that year was "Isn't it beautiful!" This mortified me at the time, but the truth is that I still go on that way about the wooded hills of northwestern Connecticut.

As the months went by that first year in Sharon, I felt more and more nourished by living in the country. When I realized that my little white writing room in Manhattan had, in effect, metamorphosed into a much larger and lighter one surrounded by greenery, I felt elated and then determined to put distractions behind me and get back to work. I remembered relatives telling me years earlier that the Vermont house I had inherited near dense woods and wild mountains was too isolated and too costly for someone my age. But after buying the house in Connecticut, I sometimes wondered what would have happened if I had defied conventional wisdom and found a way to live the life in my twenties that I finally did in my forties. I was glad I had never moved to the Southwest; the impulse was gone, played out by writing the O'Keeffe biography. A brief return to the Hamptons in eastern Long Island was my final good-bye to that overbuilt place. My corner of Connecticut had a large river, small lakes, low mountains, dirt roads, working farms, but not much else. Feeling the gravitational pull of its gentle beauty, I was relieved to take the ferry back to the mainland and drive north to what I was already calling my quiet hills, *my* hills, my lovely New England hills.

When I had seen the irises bloom, I felt as if I was born to garden. But I had still done little more than *"watch what came up where,"* as I jotted down in my notebook, and read about how to cultivate plants. A tiny garden with a brick walkway and bench outside a bookstore in Salisbury was inspiring; the day I noticed it, I became more enthralled by the arrangement of its flowers, bushes, and small trees than the books inside. Pale pink tulips blooming above blue creeping phlox looked so enchanting that when I got home, I wrote down that *"maybe I can do the same thing with yellow tulips and white arabis."* Its artistry made me aware of the importance of a mental repertoire of many plants, a knowledge of their needs, and the imagination to envision how they would look together.

There were many questions to answer, however, before I could begin. Fred McGourty assumed I needed an overall design, and I knew he was right. I remembered the question he had put to me and sketched hourglass shapes and inverse ones on photocopies of the surveyor's map, realizing that one shape allowed for more open space, while the other required more dense planting. At first I liked the idea of making a precise plan, working out month-by-month drawings on tracing paper to place over one another and study the sequence of flowering. I planned to make them to scale, like those in gardening magazines, with tidy little ovals representing trees, turf, and perennials, each one labeled with Latin and common names, height, color, and bloom time. With such ideas in mind for my garden-to-be, I allowed myself to hope that, at last, I was living in the right place.

It was almost November when the large leaves of the maple behind the house became edged with yellow, then entirely yellow, and began to float down into huge airy piles. After the first hard frost browned the green growth, I clipped the remaining iris leaves into short fan shapes and cut the grass for the last time before winter. As I worked away under the canopy of brightening foliage, it was impossible not to feel a glimmer of happiness. I was discovering that when I was worried about anything—my writing, my love life, or the yard itself—going outside was like passing through a looking glass from a darker to a lighter state of mind. Soon the backyard was covered with a thick layer of white icing again, and where sun glanced off snow the way it had on moving day, the glare was beautifully and brilliantly intense.

t w o

R O O T S

Mother took me on the
obligatory garden tour—
and this time, having a
garden of my own,
I even took notes.

June 3, 1985

PROBABLY TO MY PARENTS OR
grandparents, certainly to my
great-grandparents, it would have
looked like a timeless picture, but a
sight of amusement or puzzlement
to my city friends. There I was, in
the shade behind the barn early on
a spring morning, shoveling dirt
onto a sturdy piece of wire mesh
laid over a wheelbarrow. When the
mesh was piled high, I ran my
gloved hands over it, sifting stones
from the soil as well as walnut shells,
blackened fern heads, chunks of
bark, and from time to time a missing trowel, garden glove, pair of

sunglasses, and, once, a dirt-encrusted leather tool holder. As a few fat earthworms wiggled through the half-inch openings of the mesh, I tried not to grind them into the wire. Nearby was a huge green heap of weeds and cuttings from the garden. Another unripe pile next to the one I was using held old leaves and other browned debris topped by dried cow manure.

Dig, dump, drop the big shovel, run my hands over the humus, toss the detritus into a basket, wheel the heavy load alongside a flower bed, then shovel the loose, dark, sweet-smelling compost onto it. That morning and many others I repeated this ritual for hours, until tiredness set in, or until the cool shadow of the barn disappeared, whichever happened first. Until then I was glad to be alone behind the barn because, despite the dirt, sweat, and exhaustion, I felt completely contented, as if I were, say, making a chocolate cake.

Despite my pleasure, when I had a little distance from the sifting and the shoveling, I wondered what drove me to do it. Genes going back through the generations had evidently emerged in me with a powerful force. This atavistic instinct that had overtaken me, I assumed, was the same impulse that had compelled my ancestors to plant seeds in the spring so they could eat in the winter. I had always assumed that I possessed free will, but now I wondered if I did. In early spring, as soon as I saw pansies in a garden center, I found it difficult to drive by without stopping to search for the biggest ones with distinct dark markings on their velvety faces. Like the plants with their biological code that programs them to germinate, grow, bloom, and set seed, I felt as strongly encoded to water and weed during the growing season. All I wanted to do that spring (and all the following springs) was live by the weather—garden on dry days and write on cloudy or rainy ones. As I moved between piles of decayed matter behind the barn and the stoneware chamber pot inside, I felt a little like a wilding, as I forgot to eat or feed the dog or do much of anything else outside the garden.

Early photographs of the backyard show a handful of young plants looking skimpy and lost at the base of the barn wall, but during my second May in Sharon I noted that it was *"gloriously beautiful here—lush, green, and it's as if I'm seeing the garden for the first time."* I must have admired the growth because of all the hard labor I had put in. That spring, the first one of real gardening, I moved more than a dozen bushes and small trees—lilacs, roses of Sharon, arborvitaes, and others— that were, to my eye, in the wrong places. Over the concrete slab behind the house, I nailed down boards for a place to sit in the shade of the maple. After I lifted sod to create borders for flowers alongside the barn and picket fence, I was unsure what to plant. While I was making up my mind, I put in ground covers like sweet woodruff in shady places and annuals like marigolds in sunny spots. I also spread a large rectangle of heavy black plastic over the sunniest place in the back of the yard to kill the grass in preparation for a cutting garden. As I weeded, spread endless bags of mulch, and did myriad other tasks, I uneasily asked myself what being bodily bound to part of an acre was going to do to me, or to my writing, and whether my deepening roots would pull me down.

At first my concern about being programmed like a plant was an intellectual issue because, after all, gardening was so enjoyable. I did not want to be anywhere else. When I did go away, I found myself counting the days until I could return. As time went on, there were fewer things I wanted to do if they took me away from the garden. Nature is both a "kingdom and a place of exile" for women, in the words of Simone de Beauvoir in *The Second Sex* (significantly, using *and* instead of *or*), and I wondered if I was falling into the homebound existence of my female forebears.

As I worried about my possible "exile," I thought about whether the urge to plant was more a matter of nature or nurture. While nature as experienced in the garden appeared to have the upper hand at the moment, nurture was playing a big role, too, at least in my case. Several years earlier, on a visit to my father in Vermont near the end of his life, I was startled to see that he had given up hunting for gardening; he had cleared underbrush near his house and had tilled the soil for a vegetable garden. He had also started seedlings inside, transplanted them into tidy rows, and then carefully mounded soil around each green sprout to protect it from a cold spell. Maybe I should not have been surprised; one of his grandfathers had been born on a farm, and the other, a minister, had retired to a farm on a southern Vermont hilltop. His aunts had flower gardens, and his mother, my grandmother, Gaga, had gardened with great pride. One Sunday, before the arrival of her bridge club, she shamelessly asked me to help camouflage the bark of an ailing birch tree among the greenery behind her house in Providence with a piece of birch-patterned wallpaper.

More is known about relatives on my mother's side of my family, who, as far back as I can tell, lived in New England towns and villages, where farming and gardening were part of everyday life. One of my mother's grandfathers had a large farm in Lexington, Massachusetts, that was originally part of a crown grant; the last of the land was sold off after his death during the Depression.

I have no memory of my mother without a garden, even though she only began in earnest after her last baby was born, when she was almost forty. On spring afternoons when I returned from school, I always knew where to find her. After putting down my books, I would go around to the back of the house, open a gate, and find her kneeling on the grass in shorts, her bare hands moving rapidly among the flowers. For a few minutes I would talk toward her backside and listen to her kindhearted but distracted replies before going off to find my friends. When I study old black-and-white snapshots taken with my Brownie camera, I see grayish shapes of daffodils, hyacinths, tulips, and sharply pointed iris leaves all rising above a profusely blooming ground cover, probably a creeping phlox. Rose vines grow up the high stockade fence around the small backyard, while hostas and ferns cluster in the shadow of the house. When I put the pictures aside, what comes to mind is a dense and fragrant lily-of-the-valley bed beside the back door. I used to pluck handfuls of short stalks holding little white bells, put them in a glass of water, and take them upstairs, where their sweet smell would permeate my bedroom. Most vivid of all is my memory of an azalea bush that used to burst forth with hundreds of delicate pale yellow blossoms every May, when it turned into a beautiful bauble, like a ball of pallid sunlight, which always reminded me of the fragility of my mother's peace of mind.

Gertrude Jekyll, the grand old lady of English gardening, observed that the appeal of gardening becomes greater with age. Certainly it was in middle age when my mother found happiness in the more harmonious realm outside the house. She was the gardener in the family, and the backyard was also her arena for mastery and creativity. Probably inevitably, I began to garden about the same age as she did, after I was able to work at home. Maybe by our thirties or forties, women are more likely to have property, or time, or patience, or an itch for more self-expression that leads us to gardening. After spending years taking care of others, many mothers are perhaps ready for a quiet, private place to think their own thoughts. Other women may act from a midlife drive and desire to possess and beautify a place.

Whatever the case, the wish for a garden in middle age often has its roots in childhood. Simone de Beauvoir wrote that girls often feel happiest outside, where they are not constrained by the rules of inside; after they grow up, memories of hours spent in gardens, fields, and woods become a source of strength. Beauvoir's observation came back to me when I came across a school essay written by a teenage girl in 1920 at the school my mother and I attended. For her fifth birthday the girl had asked for a garden; it was a place of her own where she pranced around in the springtime, sobbed after being scolded, and let loose her anger. Her mother planted a hedge around it in case the plantings grew to be unsightly and, from her point of view, they did. "My garden is not at all like most gardens," the essay goes on in a triumphant tone, because the flowers "are not planted in even rows, like a nice, neat little girl's should be, but are all mixed in together, making a lot of brilliant colors when they are in bloom."

The summer my mother turned nineteen, she took a number of snapshots of her mother's flower garden in the windy seaside village in Little Compton, Rhode Island, where the family spent summers. One frames flowers and, in the distance, the family's shingled eighteenth-century farmhouse shaded by old elms where hollyhocks reached all the way to second-story windows. She also snapped a branchless tree trunk in the middle of the garden that was covered with climbing roses and topped with a large birdhouse with a thatched roof. Radiating away from the trunk was a circular pattern of earthen walkways edged with upended bricks and low boxwood bushes. When I study the blurry gray snapshots, I can just make out rosebushes, phlox, delphiniums, and more hollyhocks in the flower beds. The garden was hidden away by a privet hedge and a stone wall encircled by large evergreens and trees. The pictures give the impression of an easygoing summer garden of excellent design, a protected bower that was intended more for personal pleasure than for horticultural perfection.

My mother loved to be in her mother's garden, she told me, but she only hinted at why: it was because she spent the most time with her reserved mother there. She was closer to her genial father, whom she remembers doing little in the garden except clipping faded roses. While my grandmother, called Granny, clipped, staked, and watered, she showed my mother what to do—like deadheading a rose back to where its branch had five leaves—the way the older woman had undoubtedly learned from *her* mother during the last two decades of the nineteenth century. This great-grandmother, Grandma Godfrey, lived all her life in New Hampshire villages, and appears in photograph albums as a tiny, wiry, smiling person with big ears and wispy white hair. Usually wearing practical cotton summer dresses, she looks like a woman who knew how to use her large hands. When I asked my mother about the garden her grandmother must have had in Hampton Falls, New Hampshire, she cannot remember it, probably because as Grandma Godfrey got older she spent summers at the Rhode Island farmhouse. My mother pasted the prints in her scrapbook, along with party invitations, engagement announcements, and notices of the charitable activities of the Junior League. Did she treasure the snapshots of her mother's garden because she was already dreaming about one of her own?

After I was born, my mother often brought me to her mother's garden. My memory of Granny's garden is of a flowery domain that was always drenched in sunlight, always fascinating, and always safe. This recollection is linked in my mind to the pungent odor of the low boxwood hedge, most likely because its small, shiny leaves were at the level of my nose. I should have more memories of that garden, since I stayed in the farmhouse with my grandparents the summer before I turned ten, while my mother and stepfather remained in Providence with their newborn infant and toddler. But memory has its mysteries, particularly when loneliness is involved, and no matter how hard I try, I cannot pull up images or smells or stories or feelings from that summer except for fear of the forbidden muddy pond past the garden at the end of a grassy path.

There were more grandparents in Rhode Island when I was growing up, if I counted the parents of my stepfather. The grounds of their summer estate in Bristol, tended by Nelson, the gardener, and his helpers, swept to the edge of Narragansett Bay. The closely clipped lawn was shaded by towering trees and marked by gravel paths. I vividly remember the swing and seesaw as well as the tennis court, tall flagpole, and a bubbling birdbath that rose out of a carefully tended mass of English ivy. My step-grandmother, whose formality kept me from addressing her by name, was a petite, proper person with a tinkling little laugh and coiffured red hair going to gray. Gardening, at least when I knew her, was a matter of clipping flowers for the spacious cool rooms of the fieldstone mansion. It was in the cutting garden that stretched a hundred feet toward the bay where she picked the sweet peas that floated in the finger bowls at luncheon. In contrast to my *real* grandfather, who only removed spent rose blossoms, I noted to myself, my gruff step-grandfather liked to cut buds off bushes in the rose garden on the theory that the remaining ones would grow bigger.

When I went with my family to Bristol on Sundays, my mother made me wear a dress and tightly braided my hair or firmly pulled it into a barrette. After lunch, while the younger children played together and the grown-ups talked on the terrace, my mother used to encourage me to overcome my boredom by going exploring with my camera. I liked going into the shingled pigeon house that was full of fluttering and cooing white birds and loose soft feathers. I also used to walk down to the rocky shore and onto the dock that went out into the water.

One August afternoon, instead of going to the end of the dock as usual, I followed the rocks along the water's edge and was astonished to find myself in a small garden that was sheltered behind thick shrubbery and low-branching trees. Enchanted by the little landscape, I sat down on a large rock and looked around. Maybe the hidden garden reminded me of the children's book *The Secret Garden,* by Frances Hodgson Burnett, about a boy and girl finding their way into an overgrown walled garden with a locked gate. I remember a stone path winding over a shady hillock and, farther on, a rivulet running over a rock near diminutive flowers, and miniature trees with small, incised leaves that I had never seen before. I would later learn that I had wandered into the rock garden of an estate known for its rare plantings. During those few minutes, after all the hours spent in the gardens of my mother and grand-mothers, I understood what a garden was supposed to be: a place where a person feels better than before. That summer day I lingered there for a long time.

ONE DAY WHILE I WAS TALKING WITH A FRIEND, HE MEN-tioned my flower garden with an unmistakable touch of scorn in his voice—my *"flower* garden"—as if it were a frivolous thing, unlike his vegetable garden, which supplied him with food year-round. Perhaps he was contemptuous toward garden club ladies or believed using land to grow anything but ed-ibles was ethically wrong. I explained that I no longer planted tomatoes and had never grown squashes or any other vegeta-bles because I lacked the time to pick them, let alone "put them up," as Granny used to say. I always had a few ordinary herbs like basil, chives, and parsley, but the truth is that they never interested me as much as inedible floriferous plants. Since growing flowering perennials, even poisonous ones, satisfied my instinct to plant, maybe my urge had undergone a muta-tion. In any event, he regarded floriculture the way it was sometimes seen in the past—as a symbol of female submission.

I rejected the retrograde idea that women are instinctive creatures of nature while men are intellectual rulers of culture. And while I regarded myself as a liberated woman, I could not deny my attraction to old-fashioned, feminine blossoms, like dainty baby's breath and pale pink double peonies. So my friend's disdain aroused my underlying doubts. Also, since I did not like wasting time doing housework, how could I explain my endless hours weeding the yard? I wondered if gardening really was a capitulation to outdoor domesticity or, even worse, a kind of captivity, of the kind Eleanor Perényi has called in her book *Green Thoughts* "a floral cage." Was giving so many hours to an unpaid, private, and underpraised activity like gardening a sort of escapism or a form of female exile?

As a little voice nagged inside, I decided to look for answers in the past. Medieval tapestries, Perényi pointed out, depict noblewomen sitting or strolling within walled gardens, where they are, depending on one's point of view, either protected or imprisoned by flowery grottoes or feminine ghettos. In a fourteenth-century narrative poem attributed to Geoffrey Chaucer, *The Floure and the Leafe,* Flora, the Roman goddess of the flower, and her followers were known for idleness, fickleness, and frivolity, while those represented by the leaf stood for heroic, manly values, Jennifer Bennett has noted in *Lilies of the Hearth.* So I was glad to be reminded that Christian nuns, as well as monks, had written down common botanical knowledge that was previously passed down by word-of-mouth; among them was the so-called mother of botany, Hildegarde, a tenth-century German abbess who produced a number of manuscripts, including one about the properties of plants. Many wise women knew that certain roots, leaves, corollas, seeds, and pods healed: foxglove, for instance, was good for the heart, feverfew for a headache, motherwort for anxiety, and poppy seeds for pain. It was also known that others were poisonous, like nightshade, oleander, and the blue monkshood that grows in my garden.

Yet what my mother taught me, and what hers, in turn, told her, was more about growing decorative flowers than medicinal or nourishing plants. But she and other privileged women are influential in other ways. When she was president of her garden club in the 1970s, I brought her a newsletter of an ecological group, Friends of the Earth, hoping that she or her club would donate money and time to the cause; after all, the word *ecology,* from the Greek *oikos* for household or habitat, suggests taking care of the earth. Today my mother and millions of other garden club women, including those in the Sharon Garden Club, are converts to the cause.

My mother also mastered far more than arranging cut flowers: she created an impressive naturalistic habitat. After she and my stepfather built a house not far from Granny's old garden, she—along with a landscape designer—planned a Japanese water garden within the building's wings. Boulders were lifted in, elevations built up, a hole for water dug, and smooth beach stones spread on winding paths. A trickle of water would eventually run over a rock into a miniature pond. Evergreens and flowering trees—dogwoods, azaleas, miniature pines, and maples—were put in here and elsewhere around the house, as well as an endless number of perennials,

including an inky, dark blue bearded iris from Granny's garden (and maybe from Grandma Godfrey's, too) that grows in
my garden today.

When I visited her from New York, within minutes of my
arrival we would be walking around this garden or that, on
the path among rhododendrons and hollies that she called "the
wild area," or through the field of wildflowers in front of the
house, or in the garden suggesting mountains and lakes within
the wings of the house. What was thriving or languishing
would be the topic of our conversation, as well as where something had come from, and whether it would stay. It was my
mother's way of sharing with me what was most important to
her while avoiding more perilous subjects, like my alien way of
life in Manhattan. Before I had a garden, however, her talk left
me with little to say.

After I moved to Connecticut, she could not have been
more pleased. At the age of seventy-three, my mother found
someone to drive her in a pickup truck full of plants and furniture all the way from Rhode Island to Sharon and back.
Among her gifts were a small rhododendron named "Laurie"
and big white Shasta daises with golden centers from her garden that I put in a row along the barn. (*"Shasta daisies have
started to bloom and I think, again, they should make up that
whole border. But then what to do with the border from April
through June before they bloom?"* I asked myself the following
summer.) She kindly said nothing about the awkward shape of
the property that I wanted to turn into a garden.

When we were in my garden or hers, I became more observant and listened more intently to what she had to say. I confessed in my notebook that I felt *"overwhelmed—encouraged and discouraged"* after my visits to Rhode Island, both hopeful about what could be accomplished and aware of how much time and work it would take. When I asked my mother how to tell if a plant was in the right place, she replied, "If it looks happy." At first this answer seemed impossibly vague, but eventually I understood that it meant the overall impression given by uprightness of leaves, shade of green, and amount of new growth. Another time when I asked why we both liked making compost better than baking a cake, I understood perfectly when she offered, "Because it's outside." Whenever we ran out of words, we would begin to talk about gardening, and then everything would be all right again.

On another visit to Sharon, we drove north to the McGourtys' garden, where attractive borders of large and unusual plants grew under towering trees. My mother bought me a shrubby Russian sage for full sun; varieties of rare white lamium, miniature astilbe, and delicate-leafed hosta for shade; and three big black snakeroot plants for partly sunny places. These plants were among the few purchases that would thrive in my garden for many years. Fred did not seem to mind that I was designing my garden myself, and he good-naturedly gave me a tropical plant with a large dark red bloom that reminded him of a flower that O'Keeffe might have painted. Around that time I signed up for the McGourtys' class at the Institute of Ecosystem Studies, in nearby Millbrook, New York. Mary Ann taught it that winter and gave me an eminently sensible grounding in gardening; as she explained one method after another, it was as if pieces of a puzzle were fitting into a pattern. One evening she brought in a double impatiens that looked like a miniature pink rose, and from then on I looked for them every spring.

On my mother's summer visits to Sharon, she would immediately want to go outside and look around. Her experienced eye would see what I had overlooked, and she would gently but firmly guide me to that place, usually to prune a tree or overgrown bush; as she pointed to errant branches, I clipped or sawed them off. After a visit I might get a large package of new garden tools in the mail for my birthday or, at other times, a flimsy cardboard box leaking dirt with extra irises or astilbes and other plants she had just dug up. Some offerings from her garden did not fare so well in my colder and shadier backyard, but others did wonderfully. Once she mailed a frail meadow rue that eventually grew into a dainty giant that waved its delicate plumes more than ten feet in the air; over the years I have moved its seedlings all around the yard, so now in July my half acre is full of tall clusters of lacy leaves and spires of fluttering tiny violet flowers. Between visits she also mailed photographs she had taken in her garden of, say, a close-up of a beautiful blossom, or an entire tree covered with flowers, or a mound of pristine snow on a branch. On trips back from Rhode Island, my car would be full of flowering plants, which would then open in my garden around the time they did in hers.

WHEN I WAS A CHILD, MY MOTHER SOMETIMES USED TO ask me to carry a dripping bucket of fruit skins and vegetable scrapings from the kitchen to the compost pile, so the practice of returning verdure to the ground was familiar. Organic material, I had learned early on, is broken down by bacteria, air, and water into humus, a rich black soil. At first I dumped my weeds behind the barn because I didn't know what else to do with them. Then I built three wire enclosures near the pile for vegetation in various stages of rot. One held a heap of fresh weeds and other green matter, another would hold the previous season's browned leavings, and the third was for blackened herbage and leaf mold that was ready to sift.

I knew this was the essence of organic gardening, but as I emptied baskets of shriveled weeds, spent flowers, and wilted clippings onto the green mound, I sometimes whispered the biblical mantra "from dust to dust." I tried to remember to shovel depleted soil or toss small sticks onto this newest pile to hurry the decay along. Since I rarely had the time or strength to turn the piles the way experts advised, I tried to layer green and brown materials to speed decomposition. Once after emptying a left pit of compost, I began a new pile by forking in dead ferns and leaves that had resisted rotting from the top of the middle pile, then adding a little dried animal blood, limestone, and fireplace ashes. *"When the left pile settles, I'll add more stuff from middle one, then toss green stuff from this spring into middle pile,"* I wrote in my notebook.

Illustrations in old garden books show farmers hoeing the soil to uproot weeds and break up topsoil, and at first I did it, too. Then I heard that spreading a thick layer of mulch over the ground prevents weed seeds from germinating while letting rainwater and earthworms aerate the earth. Since I never have enough time to hoe and weed, I began to just mulch, and only a few weeds appeared among the flowers. The importance of the primordial earthworm has long been known. As the English pastor Gilbert White wrote in his charming journal about natural life in the village of Selborne in the spring of 1777: "Earth-worms, though in appearance a small and despicable link in the chain of nature, yet, if lost, would make a lamentable chasm . . . worms seem to be the great promoters of vegetation . . . by boring, perforating, and loosening the soil, and rendering it pervious to rains and the fibres of plants, by drawing straws and stalks of leaves and twigs into it; and, most of all, by throwing up such infinite numbers of lumps of earth called worm-casts, which, being their excrement, is a fine manure for grain and grass."

The second spring when I began to dig alongside the barn, my shovel hit what appeared to be an old driveway, made mostly of compacted wood ashes. It was a wasteland, a dead sea, as far as living roots were concerned—whether they were to be the tuberous roots of irises, the tenacious roots of ferns, the shallow roots of forget-me-nots, or any other kind of radix—so I knew that the impervious six-inch layer of ash had to go. I began to dig out the gritty yellowish dirt, heaving it into the wheelbarrow, and then dumping it where I wanted an elevation at the back of the yard. I removed eight or nine wheelbarrow loads of what I noted at the time was a *"sandy, ashy kind of dirt."* In other places, even where the earth was arable, the deeper I dug, the fewer earthworms there were, and the harder and drier the dirt became, until my shovel hit hard-pan, the layer of stony ground under the topsoil. The hardpan must have been there almost forever, so the stones that clinked against my steel shovel had to be glacier till. It made me ask how roots of trees were able to push their way through such impermeable ground, let alone find any sustenance there.

As I dug, I remembered when I was five or six years old and digging in the dirt behind my mother's little colonial house in Providence, probably in a childish attempt to get to China. It was the American writer Charles Dudley Warner who observed more than a century ago in *My Summer in a Garden* that even the earth in a little garden is four thousand miles deep. The thought is appealing because it makes my partial acre seem inexhaustible, as infinite as the imagination. Night soil is the euphemism for what is taken from outhouses and spread on fields in countries like China, I recalled as I worked, and as I deepened the trench I wanted to know where the old privy on my property had been, because that is where the ground would be richest. But all I found was forbidding, heavy clay soil. This happened when I cut circles in the grass in the back of the yard and lifted chunks of sod before arranging the small bulbs of purple-and-white-striped-species crocuses in the soil. As I dug hundreds of bulbs into the ground around the yard over the years, I would always find the same packed earth, whether I was planting tulips—fluted black Parrots, double pink Angeliques, lily-shaped white Triumphs—near the house, or large white Mount Hood daffodils at the end of the yard, in the hope that they would be seen as faraway white flecks from the windows.

After the pit alongside the barn was a few feet deep and devoid of large rocks that I had struggled to remove with an awl and a mallet and then roll away, I replaced the poor soil with loads of ripened compost, along with peat moss, manure, and gypsum. Unfortunately, after a rainfall a few days later, the level of the new flower bed sank lower than the lawn; this was a problem because the ground would tend to stay sodden and rot roots. Black plastic bags of something called "LaFontan's Black Gold" caught my eye at a nearby farm stand. When I brought a bag home and slit it open, I found the richest, darkest humus that I had ever seen. I heard that I could get more in a nearby town at an address that led me to a small stone house among abundant greenery in South Kent, Connecticut. I got into a conversation about the soft black soil with an animated elderly woman with a German accent, who turned out to be Mrs. LaFontan. Born near the Black Forest in Germany, she had emigrated to America at a young age and married a Frenchman. At the end of World War II, the LaFontans moved to Kent and bought seventy or so acres of land that included a large spring-fed swamp.

Their son, André, later told me about an old German saying that if you throw a pocketbook over the end of a rainbow, your wish will come true. One day when a rainbow arched over the wetland, that is what his mother did, having no idea of the riches underfoot. After a trench was built to drain the bog, she noticed that when black muck from it washed into her garden, she was able to grow prize-winning dahlias as big as dinner plates and tomatoes that weighed as much as three pounds. At first she gave away the mud in bushel baskets to friends, and then she started to sell it. After the story about the miracle mud was written up in local newspapers, scientists showed up to take a look. Their soil samples and depth measurements indicated a deposit of extremely pure decayed matter as deep as sixty feet. The scientists explained that for thousands of years everything that had fallen into an ancient lake, that later turned into limestone, had alchemized into humus.

After listening to Mrs. LaFontan's Jack-and-the-Beanstalk tale, I drove back to Sharon with many bags of Black Gold, including one for my sister's birthday in April. As I added it, along with my own compost, to the border beside the barn, the lovely loam gradually became a little higher than the grass. The perennials relished it, and I observed in my notebook that I was *"amazed at what plants do in their second year!"* In the autumn I managed to get eighteen wheelbarrow loads of sifted compost spread around the garden before it started to snow. After I put my garden tools away, I liked to imagine that underneath the snow the dark dirt was being worked around and down to roots with the help of earthworms as well as freezes and thaws. After Mrs. LaFontan died a few years later, her ailing husband impulsively sold the land, their son told me regretfully, leaving two thirds of the huge humus deposit still underground.

I sometimes wish that Mrs. LaFontan and my mother had met because they would have had so much to talk about. As my mother aged and spent less time gardening and more time looking out the window at her realm, plant forms became more whimsical and wilder. Tiny wildflowers sprouted between stones on the terrace, evoking a Lilliputian universe. Trees unexpectedly sent out branches into space. Tall meadow rue stalks waving purple clusters sprouted up ten feet in improbable places. Wisteria tendrils probed cracks between shingles. A stand of phlox invaded and choked a cluster of lilies. Columbines seeded themselves everywhere. The lacy leafage of Japanese maples shadowed the dwarf rhododendrons beneath them. Vines wrapped themselves around branches of pine trees and everything else, seemingly intent on strangling them. And there were other oddities that my mother, by necessity and choice, allowed to happen. One afternoon we humorously argued about whether a bold weed that amused her should be plucked.

We agreed that the unbridled hand of nature has its limits, and one day I moved a chair outdoors so she could sit close to an espaliered rhododendron and cut off faded blossoms. When she wanted to clip a little higher, she made an immense effort to stand up on her weak legs; she did so with such a flash of joy on her face that I remembered the way she used to be in her garden. After a few minutes she sat down heavily and uttered soft wishes about having a weed removed here or a vine trimmed there. I attempted to climb and crawl around rocks and trees and the overgrown path to obey her gentle commands, aware that her days in the garden she had tended for more than forty years were numbered.

As my mother approached the age of ninety, she spent more hours doing needlework. Instead of working outside with leaves, branches, and blossoms, she found a way to create a garden inside by embroidering the Garden of Eden on a bedspread for her canopy bed. It looked incongruous to see her muscular hands, roughened from years of gardening, delicately handle a slender silver needle and a thread, but her fingers mastered thousands of minuscule, intricate stitches of crewelwork. Over the pillows, pink-cheeked winged figures blow the breath of life toward a peaceable kingdom of wild and tame animals amid streams, hills, and forests. Fanciful trees have foliage full of flowers, or fruit and birds with elaborate tail feathers. Threads are sewn over and over one another to make tiny berries and trimmed with scissors to create bushy tails. Flowers are fantastical in my mother's stitched paradise: exuberant irises, lilies, and jack-in-the-pulpits are as large as the figures of Adam and Eve. My mother prided herself in taking liberties with the story of the original garden: a vine instead of a snake winds around a tree in her version, and while Adam tries to hand Eve the apple, she turns to pick a flower. As I gazed at the beautiful bedspread while making the bed, I saw that my mother invented another imaginary, if slightly subversive, kingdom of her own.

Learning a little about garden history, remembering my grandmothers' gardens, and watching my mother has given me an understanding of what the growing world has meant to women all along. It *does* have to do with creating ephemeral beauty after all, but it takes effort, energy, and determination to achieve it. Like my mother's formerly vigorous way of flower gardening, mine is not ladylike at all. I get dirty, bruised, and bloodied by heaving compost and digging holes in the hope of bringing forth a little beauty. Meanwhile, I maintain muscularity and stamina. Some doubt remains, I admit, about whether or not I have exiled myself in a floral cage. But instead of worrying about my lack of free will in the spring, I try to focus on how liberating it feels to follow the dictates of nature. The garden is like a taproot that grounds me but, paradoxically, makes me feel freer. Whether women are relegated to flowery bowers or linger there by choice, the green world is where many of us find solace and strength. When Simone de Beauvoir wrote that nature is to woman both a kingdom *and* a place of exile, she was suggesting, I see now, our need to withdraw into the world of nature to replenish ourselves, but not to remain for too long.

three

SHARON

The garden club went to Betty Grindrod's farm, where she divided perennials and gave us some—Jacob's ladder, a grass with light edges, astilbe, miniature white Siberian iris, a pale yellow primrose, a pink aster.

May 13, 1990

ONE SPRING AFTERNOON after I had lived in Sharon a few years, I walked into the old cemetery near my house, released my dog's leash, and let her run. I looked across a valley to a pattern of pale green pastures divided by dark hedgerows on a hillside that, as always, took my breath away. While the dog nosed about, I took the circular path around the gravestones, past a row of blooming lilac bushes, noticing that many carved surnames were the same as those of families still in town. I snapped the dog's leash back on and left the

cemetery, and walked behind the cannon-and-cannonballs
memorial to the twenty-eight local men who had died in the
Civil War. More lavender lilacs along the sidewalk perfumed
the soft April air; they were a remnant of "the great lilac
hedges" of Sharon, in the words of a Works Project Adminis-
tration writer in the 1930s. Among the earliest plants brought
by European settlers to the New World, the lilac was beloved
in New England for its heart-shaped leaves and large fragrant
clusters of bell-shaped calyxes that appear on the heels of harsh
winters and signal the beginning of spring.

I continued on Upper Main Street alongside the village
green, passing by the old colonial homes, some of them bearing
dates for the year they were built, 1780 and 1788. The mile-
and-a-half-long green had been the site of militia drills during
the Revolution and demonstrations during the Vietnam War.
As usual I looked closely at flower beds and bushes in front
and to the sides of houses, most of which appeared to have gardens behind them. Stone hitching posts stood along the way,
some with iron rings for the reins of horses. Stone steps in front
of the Congregational church and town hall had made de-
scents easier from saddles or carriages long ago. I passed the
path across the green to my house and kept on going because
the gusty breeze made the afternoon too exhilarating to go
back inside; it was one of those days when the bright air was a
pleasure to breathe.

After the sidewalk ended, I crossed over to South Main
Street, where the green became gracious expanses of grass

and trees on both sides of the road. I continued toward an eighteenth-century fieldstone manor house now known as Weatherstone. Years earlier on eastern Long Island I had heard about this Georgian mansion from a wealthy German artist who had considered buying it, until she was discouraged by the number of acres and outbuildings. The elegant old estate's imposing facade was especially handsome that day in the sparkling light. A round window near the roof looked like the eye of a Cyclops guarding the formal rose garden below, planted in a former carriage turnaround behind a lilac hedge.

On my walks around town, I sometimes felt as if I had stepped into a Grandma Moses painting. The artist's dreamy country scenes look as if they were painted nearby, and, in fact, many were done in the northern Berkshires. But it was more than the hilly countryside depicted on canvas, anchored by square houses, low fences, red barns, and white steeples that seemed the same. It was the pervasive sense of niceness, the impression of nature tamed and of man and beast domesticated. There is no nastiness in Anna Mary Moses's pretty world of green pastures, blooming bushes, neat orchards, and resplendent flower gardens. It is not at all surprising that her landscapes emerged from "memory and hope," as she wrote in her autobiography. Her words suggest nostalgia for her youth on a farm and years as a farmer's wife as well as wishful thinking. Thus her snowy winter scenes have pristine backgrounds, sometimes with glittery sparkle highlighting the whiteness. Stick figures are adorned in bright red, blue, yellow, and green as they ice-skate, gather wood, plow a field, tend farm animals, or ride in horse-drawn sleighs.

My motives in moving to a Grandma Moses–look-alike village were also a tangle of remembrance and a desire for reassurance. The question on my mind that April morning was if this picturesque place, with its hamlets of Ellsworth, Hitchcock's Corners, and Sharon Valley, was as nice as it appeared to be.

When I bought my house on Main Street, I knew little about the town of Sharon. Friends and family had been alarmed about my going off where I knew no one, but I was not overly concerned; after all, I had gone away to college and then moved to Manhattan without knowing anyone. Besides, I liked the idea of making a fresh start in this little arcadia. So the emptiness of an 1899 map of the village in the Sharon Historical Society across the green interested me. A tiny dark shape represents the library, and slightly bigger rectangles stand for churches; explicit lines delineate streets, driveways, and property boundaries. The marks for dwellings are neatly lined up along the streets like miniature pieces in a game of Monopoly. In this orderly, linear world, even the dots denoting elms on the oblong green are in straight rows. This bird's-eye perspective made the old village look like a toy town without inhabitants, or conflict and confusion, and its apparent vacancy suggested all kinds of possibilities.

Grandma Moses was hardly the first person to idealize rural America or even the township of Sharon. In the late nineteenth century, a writer named George Hepworth spent a summer in Sharon "to get a new grip on myself," as he put it in *Brown Studies, or, Camp Fires and Morals*. In a true account that reads like fiction, he recalled staying in an inn and exploring the peaceful village and surrounding hills on foot and on horseback before meeting up with a long-lost love. "Beautiful Sharon! If you have not been there you may possibly say that my language is too strong," he wrote. "From every hilltop I had a new view, the landscape being varied plains, rivers and lakes, all framed by ranges of mountains along the horizon line." He went on: "When you know all you will understand why Sharon is like paradise; and why I am building a cottage there on a hilltop just outside the village limits."

Like Hepworth, I had reason to hope that the town might have elements of paradise, which I thought of as more than a matter of beauty. Returning to New England was an act of simplification for me, one that promised to settle something inside. Around town I did not need to explain myself very much to anyone or, for that matter, to myself. I also hoped for tranquillity as well as opportunities for conviviality. My optimism was encouraged by words of the first selectman, born in town like his father before him, who had recently told a reporter for *The New York Times* that Sharon had a good blend of people, no controversies, and a conciliatory spirit. "There is no factional in-fighting," he said. "Sharon is a charming, lovely place and everybody seems to want to keep it that way."

In my wish to become a part of this perfect place, I signed

up for medical training and joined the volunteer ambulance squad, whose members came from all walks of life: there was a farmer, a banker, a handyman, a publisher, a naturalist at the Audubon Center, and a nurse at Sharon Hospital. We most often responded to scenes of accidents and homes where an elderly person was feeling unwell or had lost consciousness, and I found it gratifying to be of help. Compared with the Hamptons, the wall between natives and newcomers did not seem high. The farmer promised to bring manure for my garden (he put a large steel drum for it in the garage) and brought everyone ears of corn during the August harvest; once I gave him an armload of flowers for his wife in exchange. I liked having a beeper along with clippers on my belt when I worked in the backyard, even though it sometimes meant abandoning whatever I was doing and rushing around the corner to the fire station, where the ambulance was parked.

I also joined the small Sharon Garden Club, presided over by the kindly wife of a retired minister. The garden club was an informal gathering deliberately not associated with the more organized and social Garden Club of America. The women members at the time were hands-on gardeners—a real estate agent, a professional gardener, a garden writer, a farmer's and a doctor's wife, and a large number of elderly homemakers— who gathered to share practical information about plants, tend several plots around town, visit one another's unassuming gardens, and, occasionally, take a trip to an elaborate one, like to the fashion designer Oscar de la Renta's in nearby Kent. The club held typical small-town events, like a yearly potluck supper in a member's garden and a plant sale to raise money for its activities. For the most part, meetings were sedate, but at times there were squabbles about how much to pay speakers on topics like growing irises or orchids, and who would weed the club's wildflower garden at the Audubon Center.

At yearly plant exchanges of members' floral "extras," I acquired many of my most vigorous and prolific varieties, like forget-me-nots that miraculously fill and flower in maddening gaps in the garden, which had proven they could flourish in Sharon's cold and changeable climate. At other times the monthly newsletter offered excess white lilacs, daisies, foxgloves, and phlox, all from members' gardens. One May the founder of the club, a young woman who was head gardener at Weatherstone, invited members to her parents' farm a little way outside the village to give away divisions from the perennial bed. (When I asked her if any were by chance descendants of cultivars from the old garden at Weatherstone, she emphatically said no.) The plants I carefully put in cardboard boxes that Saturday morning and took home included the yellow primrose, white astilbe, and pale green striped grass that are still growing in my garden.

Digging holes for perennials in the backyard was like going on an archaeological dig. A few inches under the ground in a far corner of the yard, my shovel unearthed a century's remain of buried garbage: broken clamshells, old shoes, rusty metal tools, turquoise medicine bottles, and midnight-blue glass inkstands. Near the barn the shovel hit pieces of iron, possibly dropped rather than discarded, like horseshoes, square nails, bits of wire and pipe as well as chains and rods, even a heavy round weight. Iron ore had been discovered in the area more than two centuries ago; eventually, iron was hammered in forges into many kinds of tools and other items, including cooking pots and armaments for George Washington's army. One afternoon when moving daylilies to the back of the yard, I discovered a perfectly shaped, gray granite arrowhead chipped away to a sharp point. Evidently, hundreds of years earlier Native Americans had hunted on my bit of land before settlers had driven them away.

After the colonists established property lines, they set about building fences. On nineteenth-century engravings of the village, fences enclose all the gardens, presumably to keep wild animals out and tame animals in. Fences made of rough boards nailed to posts were erected near houses, while chestnut rail fences or, less commonly, stone walls marked boundaries of pastures and fields. Two hundred years ago, in a display of artistry and affluence, the large garden at Weatherstone was enclosed by pine pickets nailed to cedar posts, then the top of every picket was carved into a clover leaf shape, and the fence was painted moss green.

Fences had begun to interest me after I moved to Sharon because of those around my property. The harshly metallic chain-link fence cut the backyard in two in a senseless place beyond the barn. After staring at it helplessly for a while, I put an advertisement in the weekly newspaper offering it free to anyone who would take it away. Within a week a short, stocky, barrel-chested man arrived and pulled every concrete-encased steel post out of the ground with his bare hands, then tossed them, along with the coils of silvery mesh, into his pickup truck. After he drove away, the backyard looked much better.

While I wished to be part of the village, I wanted some privacy, too. So I had a high fence put up between the garden and the driveway and the street, but not where a neighbor's lower white picket fence stood between our yards. The neighbor, a white-haired widower who lived with an English setter, had introduced himself over the fence and offered me yellow dahlia tubers, which he had wintered over in his basement. Almost every time I went into my yard, he also went out to putter in his vegetable garden and engage me in conversation. A few years later, after he found another wife, he put his Victorian house on the market and offered me his old wheelbarrow and garden tools, some of which I still use today. It seemed a propitious time to put up my five-foot fencing on our property line. I asked if he minded if I replaced his three-foot picket fence with more of mine, and he said he did not. However, after the board-on-board fence went up (which can only be seen through from an angle), he complained bitterly, even though he was moving away.

The longer I lived in Sharon, the more I realized that the

place was no paradise. Personalities are magnified in small towns, I noticed, and a critical or angry or willful individual easily taints the mood of a meeting or public gathering place like the library. After a nasty struggle over the election of a new first selectman and issues like whether to build affordable housing for the young and the elderly, I wondered what the previous selectman had meant when he told a newspaper reporter that there were no controversies in town. I remembered reading about Sharon being affectionately described as "the heart of the world" by a minister a century ago, but now I was questioning his sentiments.

Then resentments intensified between natives and newcomers as housing prices soared. While those born in Sharon often had difficulty affording the farms and homes of their parents and grandparents, outsiders were buying them for weekend or vacation retreats. I overheard remarks disparaging wealthy weekenders, and, in fact, many weekend and weekday residents rarely mingled. Other discoveries unnerved me about my adopted town. After I joined the Democratic Town Committee, I learned that the politically conservative Young Americans for Freedom was organized on South Main Street at the family estate of William F. Buckley, Jr., when it issued what it called the Sharon Statement in September 1960. The place where I had unknowingly settled began to appear very different under its idyllic surface, and I was worried. If I started to dislike Sharon, not only would I have to leave it, but I would also have to abandon my house and garden, too.

My wish, indeed my *NEED* to like Sharon was so pressing that I started to read about its past. I wondered why the construction of a Georgian manor like Weatherstone had begun before the Revolution in a village that was only twenty years away from being a "howling wilderness," as early explorers put it, and one that was separated from the rest of the commonwealth of Connecticut by the rapid waters of the Housatonic River. When work on the house started, most other structures in Sharon were simple log or frame dwellings, so its three stories topped by a steeply pitched roof were audacious.

An ancestor of the original owner wrote a letter in 1699 about the many dangers of the Connecticut wilderness. Besides hostile "Red Skins," whom his father, a clergyman, had tried to treat with "Justice & Authority," the writer said, the other "grate Terror of our lives" was "Wolves." "The noyes of theyre howlings was eno' to curdle ye bloode of ye stoutest & I have never seen ye Man yt did not shiver at ye Sounde of a Pack of em." I was thrilled to find this vivid old account in the historical society, among other letters written by members of the Smith family, who had lived in Weatherstone for more than 150 years. Many are richly detailed descriptions of eighteenth-century Sharon, and some are full of unsettling stories about Indians, slaves, armaments, and the ravaging of the land.

In 1732, a land rush began after iron ore was discovered in the loose soil around woodchuck holes in the western highlands of Connecticut. Surveyors drew dimensions of a large township of almost sixty square miles, bounded on the east by the river, on the west by what was the colony of New York, and on the north and south by the townships of Salisbury and Kent. The new town was given the Hebrew name of Sharon after a biblical plain known as the garden of Palestine.

Mountainous near the river, the land gives way to gentle hills and valleys. (These hills were once an ancient sea, which explains why lilacs grow so abundantly here: their roots relish limestone-laced alkaline, or sweet, soil.) A settlement was established on a slope at the western border near several small lakes where the soil was most fertile, judging from the impressive height and straightness of the trees at the time. At Sharon's first town meeting, a bounty was put on wolves, and plans were made to lay out a common grazing area and a burying ground, the cemetery near my house where I like to walk. Homesteads of eighty acres were laid out along a footpath and drawn by lot. Settlers had to clear and fence in at least six acres of forest to validate deeds; they brought seeds and seedlings from towns to the east, and early gardens in Sharon had corn, turnips, squash, beans, and potatoes. Whittling down the eighty-acre lots began almost immediately. What eventually became my half acre was almost certainly stripped of mature trees and undergrowth by 1740 because it lay alongside the original footpath, which over time would be widened for packhorses, then wagons and carriages as it became known as Main Street.

Each new town in the colony was obligated to find a Congregational preacher, but it was not easy in Sharon because the large, forested, and unruly township had a reputation for irreligiosity. In 1756 the Reverend Cotton Mather Smith, a recent graduate of Yale College, arrived and remained for the rest of his long life. Parson Smith, as he was called, was "rather tall, and united great benignity and acute intelligence in his expression," while his manners had "simplicity, grace and dignity," in the words of a clergyman of his day.

The parson's brother, Simeon Smith, had studied medicine in Edinburgh. After he bought land in Sharon in 1758, it was he, inspired by great houses in Europe, who began to build Weatherstone two years later with the help of a political exile from Genoa and Italian stonemasons. Simeon quickly made a fortune importing a wide variety of goods from Europe and the West Indies, including seeds and saplings for his garden. He was, it turns out, an imaginative, ambitious, and gifted gardener. His two-acre garden was laid out on a slope to the south of the house, where there was abundant sun as well as water drainage and wind protection. The slope ended at a brook that was dammed for fish. Even so, the red, white, and purple grapevines for making wine had to be covered with earth every winter to withstand the harsh weather. His garden was unusual for its rare vegetables, like asparagus imported from England in 1773. It also had precious cherry, peach, pear, plum, and apple trees.

When Simeon's large stone house was finished, its third-floor ballroom became a town gathering place, including for a literary society that met weekly except in the growing season. It seemed to be started for the sake of Simeon's niece and the pastor's daughter, a lively and intelligent girl named Juliana, after her younger brother, Jack, went off to Yale. Her letters contain witty and insightful remarks about townspeople as well as rebellious words about the proper place of women in the years before she married a future mayor of New York City. (In meetings of the literary society, ladies were expected to maintain "a seemly silence while the slower half of creation was laying down the law," she acidly wrote.)

Juliana's letters also indicate the enormous variety and importance of early gardens in Sharon. Almost everything her large household wore or ate, from foodstuffs to flax, was grown in the family garden, especially during the difficult years of the Revolutionary War. When Thanksgiving was held in Simeon's large dining hall during the war, few imported spices were available, so dried cherries were substituted for raisins in mince pies. A wide range of vegetables was served, including a new one the girl spelled "Sellery," grown from seeds her uncle had ordered from England that came originally from Turkey; it was uprooted in autumn and buried in dirt cellars to eat raw in winter.

Her brother Jack arrived from New Haven for the holiday on horseback carrying two rare oranges in a saddlebag for his grandmothers. After graduating from Yale and becoming a lawyer, Jack married Margaret Evertson, the daughter of a wealthy Dutch landowner in nearby Dutchess County, New York. (It was a propitious match for the son of a clergyman "with no prospects beyond his Profession," in the estimation of his youngest sister, Polly.) A miniature portrait of Margaret painted on ivory shows her blond hair arranged in the high pompadour style that she wore all her life. After an October wedding in the bride's home, decorated with autumn leaves, bittersweet, and berries, the Smith family escorted the newlyweds back to Sharon in a "fine Calvalcade coming over the Hills in the Moonlight," wrote Polly. The wedding party returned to "Uncle's fine House," she continued, because Simeon had fallen into debt after the war, and sold his house to the parson, who then turned it over to Jack and his bride, before fleeing his debtors in the territory of Vermont.

One of the bride's uncles had given her four young heifers with calf for a wedding gift. Her father, in turn, presented her with "the Boy & Girl she has always called her own, Jack & Nancy by name," whom the pastor promptly married, Polly reported. Besides cattle and slaves, the nineteen-year-old bride brought an elaborate trousseau to Sharon that included seeds, roots, and cuttings from her family's estate. The two terraced acres of her new home grew vegetables and herbs for eating, flavoring, fabrics, and medicines, but no decorative flowers because Puritan tradition discouraged them. Coming from a Dutch background, Margaret also brought tulip bulbs originally owned by an ancestor in the Netherlands, where tulips had long been highly valued for their beauty. The young woman wanted a "garden-close" with flowers interspersed with vegetables, explained Helen Smith, a great-granddaughter, in an article in *The Century* magazine in 1906.

Helen Smith also described abundant flower borders backed by hedges along a wide gravel path. Margaret was proud of her ten varieties of roses, especially the one she described, echoing an everlasting complaint, as "surpassing fine, being very double and a pure, soft white, bearing abundantly; the sweetest and best of all my flowers only that the hateful rose bugs do spoil them so." After her husband, who came to be known as John Cotton Smith, served a term as governor during the War of 1812, he retired to the fieldstone "Governor's house" in Sharon and its surrounding thousand acres for the rest of his life.

Outside the Smiths' impressive garden, it was a different story. Sharon's landscape was being relentlessly stripped of its oak, elm, walnut, chestnut, maple, and other hardwoods to be burned in hundreds of pyres for the charcoal needed in iron making. The air was smoky from blast-furnace fires and brooks were polluted by mine waste; dynamite explosions roared in mines, hammers clanged in forges, and railroad trains rumbled and whistled across the countryside. In 1806, John Cotton Smith wrote that he was glad that the number of

Sharon's forges had dropped from five to three, but, in fact, the region's iron industry had not yet reached its heyday. Since the ore in the hills was ideal for making mechanisms under stress, like railroad wheels and firearms, another war would bring more people and prosperity to Sharon. The shop of A. A. Hotchkiss & Sons in Sharon Valley had made farm tools until a crippled son invented and improved deadly weapons, such as the repeating rifle and the explosive shell. He died before the beginning of the Civil War, but his brother became wealthy manufacturing cannon shells and other munitions for the Union Army.

After the war, when the iron industry waned and more farmland was depleted, townspeople left for the West in greater numbers than ever. Abandoned fields and farmhouses were overtaken by underbrush and saplings, and lilacs planted near old homesteads struggled to bloom in thickening shade. As industrialization took hold elsewhere in America, a compensatory back-to-nature movement got under way. Sharon, where woods were reclaiming a wasteland, became a destination for city dwellers like George Hepworth, the writer who likened the town to paradise. Inns and a playhouse were built and a golf course was laid out. At the turn of the century, a Methodist minister published an effusive picture book about the charms of the town, in an apparent attempt to attract vacationers. Others were not so sure it was a good idea. In winter the large colonials that stood on Main and South Main streets had few lights or faces in their windows, Edward O. Dyer noted sadly in his book about Moravian missionaries at the town's Indian Lake, *Gnadensee, The Lake of Grace,* in which he observed that "a house is not a home if it is only occupied in summer."

As Weatherstone was passed down through the family, the garden became more neglected, and the lilac hedge in front grew as high as the second-story windows. By the time Helen Smith described her great-grandmother's garden in 1906, the flowering perennials had died as untrimmed hedges grew overhead and shadowed the walkway. Asparagus had spread over the terraces, along with jonquils and daffodils, all entangled with runaway myrtle and grass. In 1915, after the death of Helen's older brother, the old manor house, most of its furnishings, and its remaining forty acres were sold. During the following decades, one of the new owners named the place Weatherstone, and the old garden was turned into a lawn.

In the 1920s a number of New Yorkers, including the critic and social historian Lewis Mumford, idealized Sharon and other New England villages as the epitome of wholesomeness. While Grandma Moses was painting her pastoral utopias, city people were arriving in the country by automobile to buy up farmhouses and the old way of life was ending. Dirt roads were paved, and the remaining farmers replaced horse-drawn plows with motorized tractors. "What has been lost is part of the touch with nature. Some here call the change progress. Some think it a further fall from Paradise. Some do not judge but take it as it is," wrote Christopher Rand, who spent his boyhood in the area, in an essay for *The New Yorker* in 1952. In Sharon, wings were put on the hospital and school, and a new firehouse was built; then a small white-brick shopping center was constructed on a carnival ground that drew the post office, pharmacy, and grocery store away from the green. It was not until the early 1970s when townspeople finally voted to create a historic district along Main Street to try to suspend in time the town's storybook look.

Another day I entered the old cemetery, where gravestones now march almost all the way down the hill, and noticed a weathered stone in the shape of an obelisk near the entrance marking Parson Smith's grave. What I had learned about the history of Sharon had enlarged the town for me. The good and the bad had given me an insight into the reason for nostalgia: a way to ease guilt and heartache. To stay in a place for a long time, it may be necessary to ignore some things and to make others invisible; perhaps the imagination has to broaden. In any event, Sharon is far less provincial than it appears, now that it is part of the electronic global village. In spite of whatever memories or hopes or illusions originally drew me to Sharon, it was far from an earthly paradise, but I wanted to stay.

SOON HORTICULTURE BECAME A BIGGER BUSINESS THAN farming in Sharon, judging from the number of plant nurseries and garden tours around town. Every spring a ritual occurs when groups of women drift in and out of one another's gardens like flocks of curious birds with large hats like plumage. I invited my younger sister, who was studying for a degree in landscape design, to join me on a tour sponsored by the historical society one year that attracted four hundred garden-gawkers. Earlier I had sent her a copy of the surveyor's map of my property in the hope that she would have some ideas about how to soften its awful shape. She had said something over the telephone about a sequence of gardens interspersed with trees, but she did not have time to put the idea on paper. For some reason I could not visualize what she meant, so I did not bring my garden up; besides, she was still in school.

It's interesting to see the private side of a public gardener, so being familiar with Lynden Miller's city gardens in Manhattan, including Bryant Park behind the New York Public Library on Fifth Avenue, we went to see hers first. I admired her puffs of pink phlox in the flower garden beside her weekend house, while my sister marveled at the variety of gates and paths leading through a clipped yew hedge into wilder areas beyond. All the gardens we saw that day revealed various relationships between owner and land. The Miller garden, with a manicured border and an uncut meadow, holds two aspects of nature side by side, but within careful limits.

Although I never saw a weed in the garden, a question arose in my mind. "Can you pull a weed in someone else's garden?" I asked my sister, hoping she knew this bit of garden etiquette from horticulture school. "If you're sure it's a weed," she replied, adding the adage that a weed to one person is a flower to another. Uncertain that she was right, and suspecting that plucking a stranger's weed is as rude as correcting his or her grammar, I suggested that it's probably okay if the weed is something obvious like a dandelion and no one is looking. But I remained unsure, since no one can really define the difference between a weed and a wildflower. We agreed that it is definitely not nice to take a seed head or snap a photograph on a garden tour without asking. Is it ethical, I went on a little guiltily, to trespass and cut down grapevines and bittersweet in a neighbor's yard that are strangling your trees? I got no reply to that question.

Next we went to the large Metz garden, since my sister was eager to see its Olmsted design. She was awed by a gigantic old white birch near the house, while I was enchanted by the little cottage from which Vivaldi's "Four Seasons" floated over the pool and gardens, amplified by speakers hidden in plastic look-alike rocks. In a shadowy, hidden garden, and everywhere else for that matter, the flora looked newly planted and mulched, unlike in my garden, where I was always weeding and rescuing plants from growing into and over one another. Nature looked definitely under control at the Metzes', where manicured gardens give way to acres of closely mowed lawn.

On our way to Weatherstone, I told my sister what I had heard about the estate. A few years earlier, a descendant of the Smiths had arrived from Texas to buy and restore the manor house and have it placed on the National Register of Historic Places. The year before I moved to town, it was sold for more than a million dollars to Henry Kravis, a New York financier, and his wife, Carolyne Roehm (whose birth name, incidentally, was Smith), who then embarked upon the biggest landscaping venture ever undertaken in Sharon. While the original garden remained under grass, flower borders and orchards were lavishly replanted, the contour of a hill was changed, groves of grown trees were put in, and three lakes—one with an island—were excavated in former farm fields. The greenhouse, tennis court, and swimming pool were renovated, and a gazebo and studio were built. A huge stable with indoor and outdoor riding rings was constructed with staff quarters, and much white fencing went up. In front, a slender female statue, *Spring,* appeared in the middle of the rose garden. Finally, a security gate was installed. Townspeople were shocked by the extravagance of the project, but said little publicly as the property became the biggest taxpayer in town.

When we arrived at Weatherstone, I remarked that the owners had divorced, and Carolyne Roehm had won lifetime tenancy of what was now the Weatherstone Corporation. I had heard that Carolyne had a place in Paris, but I had seen a photograph of her in *Vogue* running across the estate's lawn in large jewels and a purple taffeta evening gown. We paused on a bridge over the old stream, where untrimmed wisteria tendrils tried to entwine us. Then we passed stagnant ponds that were green with algae (my sister said they needed fish) outside

Carolyne's "cottage" for designing dresses, walked through a field of goose droppings and past the cutting and vegetable gardens. We finally got to the white garden, where its whites, ivories, alabasters, gray-greens, blue-greens, and yellow-greens were softened by waves of humid heat among a balance of organic and architectural elements, like tall, dark green wooden obelisks for vines. We went through an opening in a high hemlock hedge into a primeval grassy circle centered by a birch and a begonia in a lead pot. "Who waters the begonia?" I asked aloud, as we entered a manicured perennial garden. It was nature neither wild nor tamed, but enhanced by the hand of an unseen gardener.

As we went from garden to garden, my sister provided Latin names and a trained eye (noting how undulating borders and hedges reflected the hills around them), while I offered remarks about garden ambience and "the pink thing" or "the purple one." We used different words, but we understood each other perfectly. At lunch under a striped tent, we overheard talk about which garden on view that day was the warmest, and it was not about the sticky heat. We agreed that, like other gardens not tended by owners, those at Weatherstone lacked heart. The grounds were an example of overgardening, an attempt to mold and contort nature too much. I admitted that I had liked it better on an earlier tour before the latest landscaping project. But even then the gardens were not as interesting as the Smiths' sounded more than two centuries ago. Our talk covered much more than gardens that day, and my sister offered an answer to an unspoken question, remarking that touring gardens together is parallel play for women the way golf is for men.

After lunch I was glad to leave Main Street and go to Lee Link's garden high up on the side of Red Mountain. It certainly was elsewhere, maybe Switzerland, with its rustic house and wide view. Behind it, only a narrow line of hostas kept the forest away, while in front horizontal bands—stone walls, a hedge, a water garden—seemed all that kept the house from sliding down the steep slope. Hers was the only place we saw that day a decade ago without a swimming pool (it had a hot tub), and she was certainly the only owner who claimed she did all the gardening herself, often getting up at dawn to weed and water. Her battle to keep forest and field at bay has resulted in a temporary truce as well as an exquisite and individualistic balance with nature.

Most gardens in Sharon are private and never on public view. Some friends in town were about eighty when they began to plan a Japanese rock garden on the north side of their little house at the foot of the same mountain. They wanted to do it themselves for exercise and as something to create together. First they dug up soil and roots and spread a deep layer of pale gravel over the ground. Bob cut underbrush for a path up the mountain to search for rocks. He was only able to take those on sharp inclines; after finding what he called "the point of balance," he put a small stone and then another under an end, until there was enough leverage to roll a two-hundred-

pound rock into his small wheelbarrow. After he wheeled it
down the mountain, Martha decided where to place it on the
gravel. "He chose beautiful rocks," she told me admiringly.
The couple also made paths on the gravel with flat stones and
placed weathered and twisted branches like pieces of sculpture. They planted vinca under a large sugar maple and hostas,
ferns, and grasses elsewhere. Iron sculptures, including one of
a large black crow, stand among the rocks and greenery as if
slightly surprised to be still. Although deer live on the mountain, they do not venture into the rock garden, perhaps because
they fear the sound of their hooves on the gravel.

My mind's eye is full of all the gardens of Sharon, including those of other friends and garden club members. I have
seen geysers, follies (whimsical garden structures, sometimes
for sitting), and a garden designed by the renowned English
landscape gardener Penelope Hobhouse on an estate with al-
pacas and other exotic animals in the fields. There's also the ru-
mored poppy garden of the artist Jasper Johns that he
supposedly likes to tend himself. After he bought a fieldstone
mansion in the village, I watched on my walks as the grounds
were transformed into a parklike expanse of trimmed greenery behind handsome stone walls and a closed gate. Eventually
I began to disassociate myself from all the gardens I was seeing.
As I looked for insights or inspirations or ideas to emulate, it
had been interesting to see "my" plants in new arrangements
in other gardens, but finally I wanted my garden to be itself,
and I was getting closer to discovering what that meant.

four

INSIDE

━━━━◆━ ━◆━━━━

Short dark days—not even any sunlight—After this weekend, the days will begin to lengthen. . . . The first spring catalog has already arrived—and this week the camellia put forth a beautiful pink blossom. I have pots of paper whites growing everywhere.

December 19, 1986

TOWNSPEOPLE IN SHARON DID not really regard my new house as mine. Even though I owned the property on paper, old-timers persisted in calling the small colonial "the Mow house." After living in Sharon for several years, when I wistfully asked the son of a farmer when my home was ever going to be known as mine, he emphatically exclaimed, "Never!" This was a jolt, because I had felt strongly, if irrationally, that the place was mine even before I took possession of it. Why this was so, I was not entirely sure, although I think it had to do with its pleasant proportions, its placement of rooms, or some long-forgotten memory. In any event, I had no idea who the Mows were, and I wanted to know.

I was curious about the old house and had been startled when a middle-aged deliveryman edging a new mattress up the stairs cheerfully remarked that he remembered when the house was built. At the time I wondered if he meant *rebuilt,* or if he was referring to a newer part of the building, or if he was mistaken altogether, but I was too busy to think about it at the time. A few years later, however, when the Sharon Historical Society included my home on a walking tour, my curiosity was aroused again. A sign nailed to a stick outside displayed a copy of a grainy old photograph of the house with a woman in an old-fashioned long dress standing in front near an elm and a muddy Main Street. Maybe it was Mrs. Mow. The sign stated that my house had been built between the years 1787 and 1806, and it described it as a structure that had been moved from one place to another around the green.

The sign also called my home THE ACADEMY, a name I thought appropriate for a place where so much reading and writing were still going on. It was time to do a title search, I decided, and to find out exactly when it was built, why it was moved so often, and how it got its name. In the record room of the town hall, the paper trail became convoluted, so I turned to the town historian. She told me that the Reverend Cotton Mather Smith had mentioned an academy in 1800 on the corner of the main street and the old coach road. At first we thought it was my house, until 1824 documents called it "the old Academy," meaning there was another grammar school in town. The year before, a few Episcopalians had leased land on Upper Main Street to erect "a suitable and commodious building for an academy," presumably where the minister would instruct children of parishioners. This newer academy was my house or, at least, the front part of it. A clue was the later architectural style of the almost floor-to-ceiling windows. It was becoming clear that the dates on the sign for the walking tour were wrong, and the building was not a true colonial at all. A few years later it was moved across the street, and there it stayed.

On an 1872 map of Sharon, a tiny black mark represents my house with several additions; it also shows its elongated strip of land—exactly an acre—extending far in the back, down the hill, and into Sharon Valley. During the prosperous decades before and after the Civil War, the property changed hands nine times, and not one of the owners was named Mow. I learned in the historical society that an upstairs room was rented out as a meeting room for Freemasons and as a club room for girls. When I discovered that downstairs rooms were used by tradesmen, I realized the reason for the house's two front and two side doors: some had led to places of business and others to apartments. These discoveries also suggested why a little anteroom is near the most prominent front doorway: it had undoubtedly been a waiting room or a secretary's alcove.

In 1882 a woman named Jane Rowley bought the property and, with her husband, Herman, opened a grocery store inside. Perhaps the anteroom, where Herman scratched his name in the window glass, was a place to pay for purchases. Was the woman in the blurry photograph of my house Mrs. Rowley? I wasn't sure. When I inspected the photograph with a magnifying glass, however, I saw that the country woman, whoever she was, had a flower garden in front, near the door leading to the anteroom. After Mrs. Rowley was widowed in 1910, she sold the property—house, barn, and acre of land—to a woman from Maine. For years afterward the house was called the Rowley house, but it was not for the reason I thought—that townspeople were holding on to the past (like later calling it "the Mow house"). It turns out that the woman from Maine had acquired the house *and* Mrs. Rowley. When Mrs. Rowley sold her property, she had drawn up an agreement that gave her the right to use the anteroom, a living room, and an upstairs bedroom for the rest of her life. This made me believe, correctly, it turned out, that the white-haired woman with the garden in the old photograph was probably Jane Rowley, the real lady of the house, who had lived there so long.

William Mow bought the house, with Mrs. Rowley in it, in 1916. The parties agreed that the Mows would provide the elderly lady with coffee in the morning and a meal at midday. Old-timers recall the rich cookies and cakes that Mrs. Mow brought to Congregational church socials and remember Mr.

Mow as a quiet, distant, and dour man, who was a deacon of the church and the chief of the volunteer fire department for many years. Most of all he was known as a builder of Victorian-style houses around town.

It was not until I located the Mows' grandson, Bill Zeller, in Poughkeepsie, New York, that I got a few answers to my questions. He thought that it was not until the 1930s when his grandfather added classical railings and carved posts to the balconies and porches and replaced a makeshift lean-to over a front door. When he told me that his grandfather had added on to the back, it finally explained the words of the cheerful deliveryman. He also told me that the anteroom had been his grandfather's office.

Town records indicate that the Mows sold off half their acre, but there was still plenty of land left for Maud Mow's large garden. Contrary to what I had once thought after finding only grass in the backyard, every inch of the long parcel past the barn had once grown vegetables, flowers, and berry bushes, the grandson insisted. In front and to the south of the house his grandmother had bulbs and annuals, like earlier owners, and on the balconies she planted flowers in window boxes. When he informed me that his grandfather's workshop was in the old carriage barn, and used wood was piled right outside it, I understood why I had dug up so many nails, horseshoes, and other scraps of metal in my flower beds. I even learned where the old privy was, near the back of the barn. And when he went on about the packed-ash driveway that used to go through the heart of my main border, I understood why I had to do so much double digging.

Long after William Mow's death, his widow sold the house in 1971 to a dentist from Long Island and died in a nursing home shortly thereafter. Four more owners came and went before the realtor showed me the listing in December 1983. Two months earlier, a woman from New Jersey had sold it at a loss to a speculator, who then sold it for a quick profit to me. I am still surprised that so many people left my house, that it had so many owners, unknown predecessors who put in the lawn, paved another driveway, removed the stone hitching post and stepping-stone, and planted the tall bearded irises that had thrilled me on a spring night. After I had been in town for a while, I met an elderly couple who had looked at the house when it was for sale, and who told me that they had declined to make an offer because it was "all cut up" inside. Whenever they repeated this story to me, I smiled politely and stifled the impulse to throw my arms around them in gratitude for not buying my beautiful house.

Meanwhile, a few doors away, one of the most historic houses on the green was allowed to decay while its owners used it as a gigantic attic. Even though the Federal-era structure was in the historic district, the Sharon Historic District Commission's rules do not guard against neglect. The house's yellow paint was peeling away and pieces of carved trim were sagging while poison ivy wound up drain spouts, weeds sprouted in gutters, and grass grew over a brick walkway. But

with a curved Palladian window over a front door and intricate woodworking under the roofline and over the windows, it
was possible to imagine its former elegance. Its windows were
dark, but when I walked by I glimpsed a bit of green—a plastic plant?—behind a torn screen. After the owners died, the
wreck was put on the market and opened for a tag sale. Brush-
ing by broken furniture, cast-off clothes, piles of mildewed
books, and stacks of filthy long-playing records, I did not
linger until I saw a scene painted on the plaster over a fireplace:
a depiction of the place in its former glory—a great white
house as proud as a sailing ship, standing among manicured
greenery and ladies in long gowns and gentlemen in top hats.

The old house's decline made me realize how much a single building on a main street can affect an entire village. And
why a historic house is a presence more important than the
person who happens to own it. This was what made townspeople regard my home as more than simply mine—over the
years it had been the Academy, the peripatetic place, and the
Mow house. Its tall windows and big shutters on the narrow
facade had been a familiar sight for passersby as long as anyone
could remember. The Mows lived in it the longest, but there
was another reason, too, for calling it the Mow house: a gesture
of gratitude for the family's deep involvement in the life of the
town (along with a dash of resistance to newcomers thrown in,
perhaps). This became evident when Mr. Mow's grandson told
me about the day in the early 1940s when the front of the house
was draped in American flags, and red, white, and blue

bunting was hung from the highest point of the roof, along the porches and balconies, and over the front windows, as a way to honor William Mow for his many years as fire chief.

When old-timers persist in calling my house the Mow house, even though it has been mine for twenty years, it does not matter anymore. Sometimes I call it the Mow house myself. Although I have never lived anywhere longer, I understand that I will always be more occupant than owner, and my house will eventually have other owners, too. Yet the knowledge that many years ago it was built for reading and writing confirms my certainty that it is truly mine in a way, at least for a while.

ONE DAY I RECEIVED A POSTCARD FROM THE POWER COM-pany complaining about the impossibility of reading the electrical meter behind the prickly pine tree in front of the house. On either side of the pine, a scraggly yew hedge had grown so large that it was beginning to cover the windows. Something had to be done about the overgrown ornamentals. It was the daylight streaming through the big panes of glass that had originally attracted me to the house; I didn't want to block out any of it. Finally, annoyed as usual by the unsightly hedge and tall, scrawny tree, I impulsively grabbed a handsaw and sawed my way through the thick trunks of the yews. Next I asked a neighbor to take his power saw to the pine; its death was shockingly swift: it took only a few seconds to sever the trunk, toss the tree into a truck, and take it away. Without the evergreens the street side of the house looked a little stark and, well, more like a New England schoolhouse, but I did not mind. I did not believe that the building's spare and unadorned lines needed to be softened.

It was nice to have more sunlight for myself, but I also needed it for the houseplants. Ever since moving day, my two huge jade plants, which were as big as bushes, had stayed in the eight-foot-square anteroom on the southeast corner of the house. With a large window facing east and another facing south, the strange little room was very bright. That first year, as spring turned into summer and then into autumn, the jade plants settled in, happily putting forth new leaflets. When it got cold, I realized that if I kept the doors to the anteroom closed and its radiator off, I had a makeshift greenhouse.

I was glad the plants were flourishing because, by then, I had been living with *Crassula argentea* for almost two decades, longer than with any one *Homo sapiens.* Our odd coexistence began when I moved from a college dormitory to an apartment and wanted to tend something living. In a florist shop I spotted a peculiar little plant with leathery green leaves sprouting from woody brown branches. The salesgirl told me it was a jade plant, a name that made perfect sense: the cluster of thick shiny leaves on its forked stem really did resemble miniature Chinese trees carved from glaucous green jade that I had seen in museums. I paid a dollar or two for the thing and brought it home, where, like a bonsai, it suggested an imaginary landscape far larger than itself.

Before moving to New York, I had asked my mother to take the plant for a while. When I returned to Providence for my possessions, I gingerly placed the jade plant in a shoe box and carried it with me to the city. It eventually found a place on a windowsill of an apartment where it was touched on sunny days by a few minutes of strong western light. Originating in the South African desert, the succulent tolerated the lack of light surprisingly well, so I bought another. Every few weeks I watered, dusted, and turned the plants so all sides would get some sun; I also trimmed them, so they would not topple over. At times they shed handfuls of shriveled, brittle, brown leaves, but they still kept enlarging. I bought other tough varieties— an India rubber plant, a stiff snake plant, and a weeping fig—until the lacy, living filigree of leaves at the windows transformed the glare of the yellow-brick building across the street into a greenish glow.

When I left that apartment, I took only the essentials, including the smaller of the jade plants. By then it had grown so big that it was difficult to fit into a liquor box, but after having taken care of it for so long, I was not about to give up. I was worried because the thick brown branches that seemed sturdy snapped off easily, but that did not stop me, either. Among the messages I got from my estranged husband that winter was "The plants miss you," meaning, among other things, that he was neglecting them. Better them than me, I thought to myself, as I tried to put images of drooping, browning, and dying leaves out of my mind. I eventually abandoned what became the lopsided and practically leafless parodies of plants, except for the other jade plant, which was dusty but otherwise the same.

After the jade plants grew dimpled new leaves in a sun-filled room in my rented house, I was ready for a display of what a houseplant book described as the plant's rare "puffs of dainty pinkish-white, star-like flowers." When I asked people how to persuade them to produce their tiny blossoms, one person recommended more light, but direct sunlight burned brownish scabs into their fleshy leaves. Someone else suggested neglect, meaning virtually no water, so I tried that for a while. Another theory was that it took a frost to beget buds, but I didn't want to risk it. Nothing worked, so after a while I forgot about flowers and settled for enjoying the stiff arrays of green platelets.

My mother, who grew orchids, hibiscus, and other exotic specimens in her sunroom and small greenhouse, gave me a 1946 edition of a book of hers, *All About House Plants,* by Montague Free, a horticulturalist at the Brooklyn Botanic Garden, which was invaluable. She also presented me with a miniature azalea that prolifically produced white blooms all winter. Like her, I learned to force bulbs like paperwhite narcissi and amaryllis. Gradually other green beauties gravitated to the cool, light anteroom, after my garden went dormant and I started to wait out the days until spring. About the time it began to snow and get bitterly cold, a camellia would put forth pale pink petals; one winter day I counted nine blooms and the same number of buds, and scribbled *"glorious!"* in my garden notebook. There was also a fragrant English boxwood, a rounded myrtle standard, a dark green pittosporum, a silvery oleander, a thick-leafed clivia with orange blossoms, a rosemary with tiny white flowers as well as scented geraniums, asparagus ferns, and many others, until the small room resembled one of Henri Rousseau's painted jungles. Like those paintings, the tableau had a beast when my dog wandered in and became all but invisible except for two brown eyes.

In spring I took the advice of Montague Free and sank the camellia and other houseplants in their pots into the ground and put others outside, but the jade plants stayed inside. It had become increasingly difficult to fit the other potted plants back inside the anteroom after a summer of growth, to say nothing of trying to water, deadhead, and turn them toward the light. As they continued to enlarge indoors, I gave up trying to use the room's pegs for coats and hats. Once I unsuccessfully tried to rent space for the bigger plants in a commercial greenhouse for the winter. After putting an advertisement in the paper, I found someone to take the enormous weeping fig. Friends took other plants, and I drove to my sister's house, near Boston, and left the big pittosporum in her large garden room. Finally, I had no more houseplants except for my gigantic jades, which I tended a little too much. *"A jade plant fell over, so I trimmed it severely, as well as the other one, and repotted them,"* I noted one time. *"One did not need it and is in shock, a grand wilt. I'm upset and hope it recovers."*

Their massive brown trunks are now settled in virtually immovable clay planters, while their silken leaves rise above them in intricate green patterns. The jade plants and I have lived together for so long, I sometimes wonder what they would say if they could speak. We assume that vegetation has neither sense organs nor consciousness, but I remember that this is controversial. Years ago Peter Tompkins and Christopher Bird wrote in *The Secret Life of Plants* about a dracaena plant that responded with anxiety to human anger in a lie detector test, after an electrode was placed on one of its large leaves. Others researching the parapsychology of plants have found that leaves react violently to abuse and act grateful for favors; some people go so far as to say that plants anticipate human behavior and bond affectionately with their tenders. Certainly breathing on leaves douses them with beneficial carbon dioxide, while inhaling around them takes in oxygenated air. If my jade plants and I have been radiating waves of invigorating biological energy back and forth all these years, then they are more like green pets than I ever imagined. Now, after almost forty years of living alongside them, I am familiar with their fragility but also with their adaptability and vitality—the way they steadily enlarge from a stable core by continuously putting forth more glossy green ovals toward the light.

IN WINTER I SPEND MANY OF THE SHORT DAYLIGHT HOURS in my writing room, which, like the anteroom, has morning and southern light. It is where I, as if part plant, absorb day-light ravenously during the dark months. Low rays of weak sun make the shadows of bare branches dance across my hands as I work at my desk. Even on cloudy days the watery midwin-ter glow on the other side of the window glass makes me feel bathed in luminescence. It is easy to go dormant during the dark days of winter, until sunlight radiating off snow makes up in intensity for the fewer hours of daylight. One February day I wrote in the notebook that, *"It's deep winter—several inches of deep very white snow everywhere—trees, rooftops—brightening this gloomy time of year."* There are other wonders to experience from inside, as well. Snowstorms often make the outside look like the interior of a glass ball that, when shaken, becomes swirling white fluff. Through the south windows I can also see the first delicate lavender crocuses push through the sodden grass in early spring.

When I was ten, I was pleased when my mother allowed me to pick out wallpaper for my bedroom. My choice was a dense yellow pattern of cute cottages with a plume of smoke coming from each chimney. Unfortunately, from the moment the intricate wallpaper was put on the walls, I disliked it in-tensely. At that age I had no way of knowing that hundreds of little houses repeated on all four walls of a room would create a feeling of unbearable frenzy. This early disappointment made me intolerant of wallpaper, as well as flowery walls, fab-rics, and dishes, for that matter. To this day I do not like to see flowers anywhere except in works of art, in the ground, or in vases and pots.

Fourteen different wallpapers covered the walls of my house when I moved in; from the kitchen I was able to see as many as six discordant designs in as many rooms. In an attempt to eradicate the imprints of previous owners and impose my own, I began to rip off wallpapers in winter months and paint the old plaster walls pure white or pale colors. As I stroked the walls with a paintbrush and pigment, I felt that what I was doing to the house's interior, I was also doing to my own insides—creating a new feeling, one that was calmer and brighter than before. The house was a pleasure, a reassuring presence, even embracing in a parental way. I remembered that Edith Wharton had written that the rooms of a house resemble a woman's nature, each one leading into a more private place inside. After I'd lived in the house for a year, only a few patterns remained, and I intended to get rid of all of them before the snow melted and I was able to garden again.

After a room was painted, I would rearrange furniture against the plain walls, including the Chippendale-style mahogany corner cupboard that my father had made. The graceful cupboard hovers in backgrounds of grayish Christmas photographs—where I am a pale bundle in my father's arms and then a toddler squirming in my mother's lap—taken on his holiday leaves during World War II. In the picture album my mother's black script identifies snapshots from the early years of their marriage—including one taken proudly of the cupboard by itself—before the book goes blank at the end of the war. When my father left home for the last time, he left the corner cupboard behind for me.

After his death, a letter was found in his safe-deposit box that he had sent to me on the eve of his departure for the war in the Pacific. He wrote of many things, among them what he called his "appreciations" of antiques, and old houses, and his wish that I might like them someday, too. "If you can truly love those things," he had written, "all the other things will fit into the pattern and your life will offer you the same feeling that is sometimes gained when reading a beautiful piece of literature." When I first read those words after moving to Sharon, I discovered a sensibility and sentiment in him that I had never known before. The cupboard still stands in my dining room, an everyday reminder of balance and grace in its grooved scrolls, arched panels, and silky wood grains. I chose a very dark shade of green for the wall above the wainscoting in the room, and I added paneled window shutters and carved ceiling moldings. Some winter day I will get around to painting the cupboard's innards, finally covering the faded yellow paint that my father applied more than sixty years ago. I had, indeed, fulfilled his hope that I would also admire traditional designs.

In winter, after bright holiday lights came down, brilliantly colored garden catalogs appeared in the mailbox. On cold, dark nights the lavish pages that heralded what now looked like an imaginary world became my bedtime reading. Glossy page after page of blooms without a blemish persuaded me that the lifeless landscape outside was temporary, and that it would become fully pigmented once again. It is when I also looked at photographs of the prior summer's borders; at the time I took the pictures, I believed I was getting the flower beds at their best, but the prints—devoid of the pleasure of being outside—tended to expose the garden's imperfections.

As I uncovered flower beds in the spring and discovered what was lifeless and what was sending forth green shoots, it was natural to think about what to move, what to get more of, and what to throw out. Even though I had made a garden plan, imposing my will on nature was not easy. Some perennials had their glory days until a bitter winter or a dry summer or the expanding shadow of the maple killed them. As sunny beds became shady, I lost a snow-in-summer beside the basement door and a double white clematis on the nearby fence, among others. One August I tried to plug visual holes with white snapdragons. *"I have too many of one thing instead of masses,"* I noted in exasperation in my garden notebook, remembering Vita Sackville-West's advice about "massing instead of dotting" with flowering plants in a border. *"I need to take out Shasta daisies except against fence, and the phlox, a lousy cutting flower. Yellow snapdragons are stupid. I never cut them. I need more little evergreen bushes."* Meanwhile, the borders behind the barn suggested a faint hourglass, but I wanted an inverse shape that would open and narrow and then open again; in any event, the curvaceous pattern was ruined by the squared sides of the cutting garden.

Despite my attempts at planning, it was warfare in the garden. Invasive plants charged ahead while reticent ones vanished. Once when I was away or inattentive, a purple lamium completely overran a low-growing azalea; I thought the azalea had died, until I discovered it one day when weeding. Dark, sinewy roots of tall ferns vigorously thrust their way under the grass, so I tried to dig up many of them with a long-bladed shovel before the fronds uncurled from their coarse brown sheaths. Otherwise the ferns would march all the way across the yard and into the woods. Gardeners, I learned the hard way, have to be wary of gifts from other gardeners, who naturally give away what they have in abundance. Most of the runaway gooseneck loosestrife from my mother, of all people, has to be ripped out every year to stop its demonic pinkish roots from ramming their way all over the cutting garden. Luckily, I do not need a steel shovel to edit the forget-me-nots that pop up everywhere since they are easily uprooted. While the aggressive roots of a mint plant are safely confined by a pot, the lily-of-the-valley and pachysandra fight it out in a scraggly war zone under the maple.

A mostly pastel and dark green garden near the house would make the backyard a peaceful refuge from garish commercial colors elsewhere, I decided. It would be ideal to have pale yellows in spring give way to a palette of pinks, purples, blues, and whites in late spring and summer, and then deeper hues in autumn to harmonize with the foliage. It was difficult to adhere to the color scheme since flowers do not obey rules, but neither, as a matter of fact, do I. I kept perennials inherited from others (bearded irises of many hues), ordered impulsively (fringed purplish-black parrot tulips), planted bulbs shipped by mistake (dark gold instead of cream-colored crocuses), accepted gifts (red primroses from my sister), fell for robust native plants (golden black-eyed Susans), bought undifferentiated annuals (yellow snapdragons), and gave in to plants' timetables (a rosebush kept putting out pink buds well into October, when I was ready for orangey tones; *"the orange chrysanthemums have come out, but the pink roses are still blooming,"* I scribbled in frustration). My garden, or any garden, I thought, has enough vitality without the restless vibrations of red. So every May, when a lone red tulip persistently, amazingly, shoots up like an exclamation point among the pachysandra under the maple, I clip it for a bud vase. And even though I tried to carefully label irises by color during their brief days of bloom before transplanting them, inevitably a pale blue blossom would open jarringly among a cluster of purples.

Gradually I added more yellow to the pink and blue bed. Once I came home with bright yellow pansies that bloomed away in the barn while it snowed outside. *"I was desperate for some bloom,"* I noted, even though I knew they would get scraggly by summer. One late July when yellow lilies from a garden club swap were the only flowers blooming in the garden, I moved them from the back of the yard to the border near the barn. Then I added a pale yellow coreopsis that blooms almost all summer after repeatedly losing a similarly bushy white baby's breath. The color of sunlight was too ecstatic a color to exclude.

f i v e

WORDS

Days seem mixtures of immense and intense mental work on the manuscript, the unbelievably hard physical work in the garden. Need both. Each counteracts the effect of the other. I hurl myself into one, then the other.

May 18, 1988

ONE JULY DAY AS I WAS transplanting flaming orange Oriental poppies with fringed black hearts—I had inadvertently bought the kind that Georgia O'Keeffe had lovingly planted and painted many times in upstate New York—from the middle of the garden, after they had turned into a tangled mess of brown, scratchy stems, I was wondering to myself why I had really written her biography. I had been motivated, I decided, because I had faced some choices similar to the young O'Keeffe's, and I had wanted to find out, to *feel,* where they had taken her, and whether she had any regrets. It had been fascinating to research and write the book, and I had found out a great deal, yet during that time I had half joked about being jealous of her adventures in the Southwest, while I spent all day, every day, sitting at my typewriter.

That afternoon I was struck by how much more gratifying gardening was than writing. I was by then at work on a second biography, about the artist Louise Nevelson. When sitting at my desk in the mornings, it was difficult to banish thoughts about the garden. Questions would intrude: Would it be too warm to weed the sun bed in the afternoon? Should I put a straw basket over a newly planted chrysanthemum to shield it from the hot sun? Maybe a pot of scraggly pansies should be moved into the morning light. As my fingers played over the plastic keyboard of my computer, they itched to be holding the wooden handle of a rake or tying up tendrils with soft twine. I struggled to keep my mind on the manuscript, because if I ventured outside even for a few minutes, the effortless work of the garden would absorb me in a heartbeat, and it might well be the end of a morning of writing.

Usually we go along locked into one mind-set or another, and it is not often that it suddenly shatters as doubts rush forth. This is what had happened on a warm spring day a few months earlier after dutifully going to lower Manhattan to interview Nevelson again. I rang the doorbell of her building and climbed a steep flight of stairs to a shadowy room, where dark wooden shutters filtered out the daylight. After chatting for a few minutes, I began to ask her about the years when she was the freewheeling "beautiful girl" described in the composer Ernest Bloch's 1933 diary. Nevelson was alternately guarded and vulnerable, and her darting, burning, dark eyes turned haunted or amused as I gently probed her memory. Though willing to answer most of my questions, she was much more interested in her work-in-progress than in the past. When I finally turned off my tape recorder, she stood up and excitedly took me over to a dim corner to see her latest creation—a coal black wooden assemblage illuminated from within.

After I descended the staircase and walked back out onto Spring Street, the hot golden light of late afternoon exploded in my face. Something about the sculptor that April day made her seem to be just another anguished and exuberant soul instead of a persona worthy of a lot of attention. Walking along the gritty sidewalk, a wave of nausea rolled over me as I tried to banish an unwelcome thought: the certainty that I was wasting my time in the city. As I passed cafés and shops on the way to the subway station, smelling the acrid scent of garbage and the sweet aroma of cut flowers, I felt, with a sense of urgency, that I should be in my garden. There the big purple crocuses and clusters of pale daffodils were at the peak of their beauty, blooming among the flowering, speckled-leafed lungwort. Oddly enough, my perception on that afternoon was not unlike one of Nevelson's forty years earlier. At a tedious meeting of an artists' organization, she had impatiently remarked to a friend that she should be either in bed with a lover or in her studio making art.

The unsettling experience on Spring Street was partly about the allure of my garden, but it was also about something else. I found it difficult to get absorbed by Nevelson's story because of her attitude toward nature, which was epitomized for me by her so-called garden. Years earlier, in the lot behind a brownstone, she had created an unnatural garden, using old junk to satirize the idea of a garden and, I suspected, even nature itself. In a corner she nicknamed "the farm," she constructed a red, barnlike structure, nailed driftwood and other pieces of old wood to it, and added a white picket fence. She also splashed orange, blue, white, and pink paint on the flagstone stepping-stones, as if to represent flowers. Before she was done, she stuck sharp-edged sculptor's tools like files and calipers, along with egg beaters, spatulas, and wooden spoons, in rows in the dirt. The way she arranged bits of broken mirror face-up on the ground to reflect the sky, as if light emanated from the earth, was interesting, I had to admit. As I worked on the biography, I tried to keep a writerly objectivity, realizing that her mocking antigarden was in its own way original, witty, and appropriate for her. Nevertheless, it irritated me.

When I had begun the Nevelson book, I was determined this time to balance a biographer's necessary, if unnatural, preoccupation with another person's story with a full life of my own. But now the biography was taking too long to write.

One reason was related to the research, but there was another as well: gardening was devouring what used to be my afternoon and weekend writing hours, while at the same time satisfying my creativity and drive for accomplishment. I had anticipated that the country would be a better place to write than the city—I had written in my journal before moving to Sharon that all I needed was a peaceful year to complete the manuscript—but now I was not sure.

I asked myself how to weigh the easy pleasure of gardening against the more elusive satisfaction of writing. And how to compare the private playfulness of growing flowers with the public experience of being published. At moments I questioned whether I should be writing at all. The act of writing demands withdrawal, and during working hours the willful virago within has to banish what Virginia Woolf called the angel of the house. Then the writer must close her door, refuse to talk, and ignore the telephone. Even worse, this creature sometimes needs more than a few hours to herself—sometimes she needs two or three days alone. It must be she, not me, I liked to believe, who at times imagined a simple life of solitude that is free and a little wild.

On days when I questioned whether art should serve life or life should serve art, I fantasized about becoming a full-time gardener. I was intrigued to learn that in the late 1930s, William B. Harris, an editor at *Fortune* magazine, and his wife, Jane Grant, a reporter for *The New York Times,* bought a small barn in nearby Litchfield for a weekend retreat from the city. "The idea was to have 'a little place in the country' to which we could bring our work, and where we could vacation," explained Harris thirty years later, writing under the pseudonym Amos Pettingill in the foreword of the 1966 edition of "The White-Flower-Farm Garden Book," the catalog of the famous nursery the couple started. "We were writers, and it seemed reasonable that writing could be done as well in the country as in New York City. Other people did it. We did it. But for me, trying to write in Litchfield County was torture, for nature beckoned so seductively that I spent far more time with her than with my work."

The uncomplicated sense of rightness I had while weeding and clipping continued to make me ask if I was in the wrong line of work. Gardening felt like a natural activity, but the effort exacted by writing often felt abnormal. And while writing emptied me out, it was gardening that filled me up again. Furthermore, every spring I was sure that I could happily spend the entire growing season searching for new specimens, going on garden tours, attending gardening seminars, digging more beds, planting new perennials, and undertaking various projects, like putting in a row of boxwood or peonies around the cutting garden, something that I never got around to doing. Brochures often arrived in the mail offering classes in horticulture, and I was well aware that I could learn to make a living by planning or tending other people's gardens. Yet giving up writing would mean abandoning something that had been very important to me for many years. The idea aroused such turmoil that when it arose I tried to evade it by throwing on old clothes and going out into the backyard, where everything was evident again.

I WANTED TO READ ABOUT WRITERS WHO GARDENED, SO one rainy Saturday I drove over the mountain and down to a covered bridge across the Housatonic River and into the hamlet of West Cornwall, where there was a secondhand-book store with a reputation for having an excellent horticulture collection. In a stark, gray clapboard building (a former scissors factory) I encountered the owner, Barbara Farnsworth, an older woman with reddish hair piled on top of her head and blue eyes sparkling behind spectacles, who exuded excitement about the gardening books she reads as literature. She admitted that she also peruses them out of what she called "peeping Tomism," a curiosity about how fellow gardeners cultivate their gardens as well as confirmation of her practices in her own garden, a place where she struggles for serene formality, she told me, structured by evergreens, that is attractive in wintertime.

On a table in the bookstore were old books with pleasing titles, like *The Summer Garden of Pleasure, English Pleasure Gardens, The Lure of the Garden,* and *The Charm of Gardens.* In a locked rare-books room upstairs, I found a first edition of a Gertrude Jekyll volume, an early garden book called *The Gardener's Kalender,* a version of Carl Linnaeus's seminal book of plant classifications, and a leather-bound volume with engravings and marbleized paper of Gilbert White's *The Natural History and Antiquities of Selborne,* where there is the account about earthworms. After telling me she often reread *The Country Garden,* by Josephine Nuese, who had gardened in nearby Lakeville, Barbara wrapped it in heavy brown paper for me and tied it with string. I, too, would flip through it almost every year, glad to be reminded of its down-to-earth suggestions, like not mulching peonies in winter (since their tubers need to be frozen for many days for the plants to bloom well in spring).

I noticed that hers and many other garden books are organized month by month, demonstrating how tasks in one season lead to those in another. The genre of garden writing stresses practicality in small spaces, I noted, while nature writing emphasizes the appreciation of larger landscapes. I also detected a gender difference: horticulture was almost always in the women's sphere, while landscape design was usually the province of men. At Sissinghurst, for instance, Harold Nicolson designed the patterns of the garden, while his wife, Vita Sackville-West, selected the plantings. Something else disturbed me. Although Vita wrote wonderfully about gardening for fourteen years in *The London Observer,* she, as well as others in her circle, disparaged her journalism as less serious and prestigious than her fiction and poetry. Her lengthy poem "The Garden," which she slowly wrote during the difficult years of World War II, expressed her sense of hope, as experienced each spring in the garden. Disappointed by the poem's reception, however, she never wrote poetry again after it was published. Instead, she started the newspaper garden column, writing it on Sunday mornings in her study in a sixteenth-century brick tower with twin turrets, part of a ruin of an old Tudor castle, which stands in the middle of the property like a gigantic garden folly. It was her choice to remain near the garden at Sissinghurst for the rest of her life, instead of following her diplomat husband abroad.

As I browsed the bookshelves, I became especially interested in writers who gardened in the harsh climate of New England, like Henry Wadsworth Longfellow, Edgar Allan Poe, and Harriet Beecher Stowe. Interestingly, Herman Melville grew corn and potatoes and harvested hay in western Massachusetts far from the sea while writing his whaling saga *Moby-Dick*. Nathaniel Hawthorne wrote in *The Old Manse* about a garden he tended for an hour or so every morning and returned to admire throughout the rest of the day. He would, he wrote, "stand in deep contemplation over my vegetable progeny with a love that nobody could share or conceive of who had never taken part in the process of creation. It was one of the most bewitching sights in the world to observe a hill of beans thrusting aside the soil or a row of early peas just peeping forth sufficiently to trace a line of delicate green."

Emily Dickinson had studied botany like other young ladies of her day; when she was a schoolgirl in the 1840s, she had pressed more than four hundred dried flowers into a herbarium. At the age of twenty-five she took over her ailing mother's large flower garden on the family's fourteen-acre farm in Amherst, Massachusetts. It was an informal garden of both wild self-sown and rare hybridized flowers; in her poems and letters, she mentioned as many as seventy-two varieties, including wildflowers, which she grew and knew. She did most of the deadheading but was too frail for the heavier work of digging and pruning. Off the southeast side of the family's brick mansion, her father built a small conservatory with walls of panes of glass and a Franklin stove so she could pot and tend orchids, camellias, gardenias, jasmine, and other tropical plants during the long New England winters.

The garden was surrounded by a high hedge and had a summerhouse, where Emily could sit unseen, observe, and write. Writing poetry and cultivating flowers were so intimately intertwined for her that it is difficult to imagine one without the other. "This is a Blossom of the Brain," is the way she began a poem, and she repeatedly found inspiration in the determination of a flower to bloom. Since both poetry and gardening demanded her ideas, persistence, vision, and mastery of form, they inevitably enforced each other.

The garden also gave her poetry a great deal of imagery, activity, and meaning. Emily often used garden incidents in poems, like exploring the significance of swiftly cutting down the last dahlias, chrysanthemums, and other fall flowers before a frost. In "the garden within," as she called her imagination, flowers were anthropomorphic personalities that represented friends and family: her mother, for example, was the tall, deep red, late-summer wild cardinal flower that attracts humming-birds. She, in turn, was the daisy turning toward the man she loved like the sun. Emily also admired the various characteristics of flowers, like what she perceived as the bravery and humility of a clover. Cycles of budding and blooming in her botanical cosmos provided innumerable insights about life and death. She understood both the ephemeral and eternal nature of flowers, the way a bloom is brief but is replaced by more flowers the following year.

In that era, it was more acceptable for a woman to be a flower gardener than a professional poet; in her lifetime she was, in fact, better known as a grower of flowers. To write she required an interior and insular way of life, and some scholars have suggested that the ordinariness of gardening activities was an anchor that empowered her to create daring and disquieting poetry. Certainly she used gardening as a common language with others in conversation and letters. Her cut flowers were also stand-ins for herself. When she did not wish to visit or see a visitor, she would send a bouquet, a lone blossom, or a flowering branch from the garden wrapped in wet paper, tied with a ribbon, and placed in a box, often along with a poem rolled up in a ribbon.

Celia Thaxter, a popular late-nineteenth-century poet, is remembered for her second and last slim work of lush prose, *An Island Garden,* about her cottage garden on an island off the coast of New Hampshire. The daughter of a lighthouse keeper, she married and moved to the mainland, where she had three sons at a young age. The Thaxters returned to the treeless island in the spring to help with her family's inn. Celia liked to go out at daybreak to clip flowers to bring indoors and better "admire and adore their beauty," as she put it, arranging them by color along a wall called "the altar" for visiting artists, writers, and musicians. Her summers sounded idyllic, but I was saddened by her story. In late middle age she set everything aside to finish work on the book, what she called her "true likeness of my wilderness of bloom," which was to be illustrated by her friend Childe Hassam. A few months after its publication, she unexpectedly died before fulfilling what I feel was her potential as a writer. An editor had hinted that her prose was as untamed as her garden, but she also had difficulty with the angel of the house. "If her life had been less intensely laborious, in order to make those who belonged to her comfortable and happy, what might she not have achieved!" eulogized her literary friend Annie Fields.

And then there was Edith Wharton, who in her autobiography, *A Backward Glance,* was nostalgic about writing and gardening in her forties at the Mount, a magnificent thirty-five-room mansion that she built in 1901 with inherited money. It was located on a former farm of more than a hundred acres of fields and woods overlooking a lake outside the village of Lenox, Massachusetts, "the real country," as she described it, where she and her husband intended to live half the year. There she was able to avoid the demanding social expectations of her class and time and do more writing, at least for a while, because of the household's "order, tranquility, stability." She designed the upstairs rooms to protect her morning writing hours, enabling her to pass from her bedroom, where she wrote, to her bathroom and sitting room without going into the hallway and encountering her frequent houseguests.

Her ability to write well in the country interested me intensely, especially after I discovered that her love of gardening had deepened in what she regarded as her "first real home," where she wanted to live for the rest of her life. Her devotion to summer flowers also surprised me, since she greatly admired the formality of relatively flowerless Italian gardens with their emphasis on marble, water, and evergreens. "The Italian garden does not exist for its flowers; its flowers exist for it," is the way she began her book *Italian Villas and Their Gardens,* which she wrote while laying out her gardens at the Mount. "My flowers are a joy," she wrote a year or so later to a friend, Sara "Sally" Norton, in July 1905, one of the summers she won many prizes at the Lenox Horticultural Society flower show. She was exultant when her "red garden," as she called it, was "a mass of bloom" of many varieties, like "annual pinks in every shade of rose, salmon, cherry & crimson," near a circle of white petunias around a dolphin fountain.

After a morning of writing, Edith would dress and walk in the sunny flower garden and the shady walled *giardino segreto,* which were joined by a straight walkway lined with linden trees. Like other wealthy women of her day, she oversaw a head gardener and his helpers, who tended the ornamental and vegetable gardens as well as the plants in a greenhouse; whether because of propriety or inclination, her interest in gardening was much more an emotional and intellectual exercise than a hands-on activity. She must have deadheaded once in a while, however, since she asked a male guest she disliked (later he was a biographer who called her a demanding and dominating mother of her flowery offspring) to do the unpleasant task of plucking faded petunia petals from their sticky nectar.

She wrote her first bestseller, *The House of Mirth,* in her bedroom overlooking the red garden. In her diary, however, she seemed as proud of her first prizes in the flower show as the number of weeks her novel sold well in New York. When she returned to a beautifully verdant Lenox in the spring of 1911, she confessed to her close friend Morton Fullerton: "Decidedly, I'm a better landscape gardener than novelist, and this place, every line of which is my own work, far surpasses *The House of Mirth.*" Whether or not she was serious, the work of writing must have seemed more arduous than watching a garden grow. In any event, and not unlike Emily Dickinson, she likened her creativity to "a secret garden," a place of inner fecundity where ideas for her fiction took root.

As I reflected on what I had learned as a result of visiting Barbara Farnsworth's bookstore, I realized that gardens were important to writers in differing ways. Vita Sackville-West and Celia Thaxter eventually gardened more than they wrote, while Emily Dickinson and Edith Wharton apparently kept both in balance.

MORE THAN FOUR YEARS AFTER MOVING TO THE COUN-try, I was at last working on the final draft of the Louise Nevel-son biography. By the end of summer, I was writing morning and afternoon and forcing myself to ignore dahlias that needed to be dug up and brown stalks that needed to be cut down. Be-fore long the stress and many hours' sitting at my desk threw out my back and forced me to slow down; after I began going out in the afternoons to gingerly rake leaves, my back gradu-ally got better. It was a lesson that I had to learn over and over again. When the garden went dormant, there was a loss of pleasure but more time to write, I would tell myself. Until, that is, the dark days inside drained my energy, resulting in less writing.

In anticipation of being able to garden full-time after the manuscript was finally sent off, I had ordered five hundred bulbs from a wholesale catalog. Warm days of Indian summer arrived, but I acted as if still on deadline and tried to plant a hundred bulbs a day. My frenetic pace was also a way to fill the sudden expanse of time and avoid the letdown of finishing writing a book. As I pushed bulbs underground, it was impos-sible not to inhale the earth's rich aroma. Planting bulbs is a supremely optimistic act, because it assumes their blossoming in the spring. I put bulbs of the delicate white Thalia narcissus along the woods to look like woodland flowers, and pale yellow double daffodils, called "Cheerfulness," on the south side of the house, where they would open early. After covering the bulbs with dirt, I placed wire and then rocks over them to discourage chipmunks and squirrels from getting them. While digging hundreds of holes with a narrow trowel, I tried to visualize how the flowers would look on publication day in the spring, until I threw out my back and came down with a cold. Instead of writing or gardening all day, it was evident, again, that it was best to find a balance between them.

After the biography was published, the land greened up. Ruffled pink tulips burst open in early May, harbingers of the double pink peonies that ruptured their green hulls a month later. I had time for trips with friends to nurseries to look for the perennials I had seen in catalogs. Whenever someone innocently asked me if I was going to write a third biography, I became unreasonably irritated. Sometimes I would patiently reply that copyright law about fair use of written materials had made research more difficult, and for that reason I did not want to undertake another one. It was startling that spring to realize that I never asked myself if gardening was worthwhile, the way I had questioned writing that day on Spring Street. But the more I gardened, the more I wanted to write from the root, or, to put it another way, to only write about what mattered most to me. The real reason that I resisted writing another biography was that I was no longer able or willing to experience another life vicariously, and I was ready to write about my own.

When I first began to garden, I had also started to record what I was doing outside. As if only growth in the garden mattered, I obsessively covered page after page with cramped script and minutiae about woodchucks, double digging, weeding, watering, deadheading, dividing, staking, edging, mulching, what I planted and moved, what was blooming or flourishing or languishing, when it rained, when I watered, when I emptied a compost pile and started another, and much more. My notes on narrow-lined, loose-leaf pages exude a great deal of excitement as well as shock at all there was to do—and how much I was heroically doing.

"Gardened all day," I wrote one April. *"Weeds in disturbing abundance north of the driveway despite three bags of mulch. The display of mostly yellow tulips and blue grape hyacinths in the grass is really quite beautiful,"* and on and on in a kind of shorthand to myself. *"Gorgeous at last and two full days of real gardening,"* goes a May entry.

Widened bed under maple, and added humus, fertilizer, gypsum, peat, and manure to it. Extended compost pile and turned it. At last have some compost to use. Finished winter cleanup and fertilized iris, day lily beds. Tried to revive grass under maple by raking up struggling grass and putting down compost, peat moss, fertilizer and grass seed for deep shade. Moved five or six meadow rue to sunny bed where hollyhocks used to be. . . . White Flower Farm order came. Although it was raining lightly, I planted everything except the lilies because they required double digging. Took four hours. . . . What's blooming: in front, iberis, another kind of blue iris, pink tulips hanging on. Iris are huge and gorgeous, all peonies are open, the oriental poppies have opened with two blooms and dozens of buds, as has one pale blue delphinium. They now reach the windows of the barn!

Writing everything down helped me learn rapidly and with recognition much of what I must have instinctively known. My rural ancestors had understood, of course, that to sow in the spring led to survival in the winter. Henry David Thoreau sounds naive to me when he writes about what he called his "curious labor" the summer he tended a vegetable garden with seven miles of rows. "What was the meaning of this so steady and self-respecting, this small Herculean labor, I know not," he wrote in *Walden*. "I came to love my rows, my beans, though so many more than I wanted. They attached me to the earth, and so I got strength like Antaeus. But why should I raise them? Only Heaven knows."

At times I kept better track of my plants than my psyche, as if the drama in the garden was a way to evade dilemmas elsewhere. Even so, every spring, after the garden was buried under snow for three or four months, I developed amnesia about what was where, including bulbs I had planted only a few months before. It was like forgetting what I knew about love and work, what I had learned from experience; it was a dangerous kind of forgetfulness, because it often lulled me into making the same mistakes again. At first I rarely took the time to reread my garden notes, but when I did, I was glad. They reminded me what or what not to do (put down soaker hoses before growth gets under way), and reassured me that I was not too far behind (the previous spring I had not put down mulch until much later than this year). I noticed the way a garden grows faster or slower, or stops growing altogether, depending on the weather. I also noted the way perennials that go dormant during the winter sometimes return stronger in the spring. When my notes reminded me of a plant that had not reappeared by April, I was interested to see how little the death mattered since gardening is rejuvenating whatever the result. Optimism overrules pessimism because every spring is an opportunity to start again. Going over my notes made my memory better, and remembering eventually made love and work go better, too.

One weekend when I was browsing in Barbara Farnsworth's bookstore, a yellowed clipping from *The Literary Review* fell from the pages of a book. "Gardening is the best, perhaps the only, literary recreation," an anonymous author had written, evidently a gardener as well. "Good writing is always a breaking of the soil, clearing away prejudices, pulling up of sour weeds of crooked thinking, stripping the turf so as to get at what is fertile beneath." Although once I had thought the opposite to be true, I then saw many similarities between the rules and routines of writing and gardening. Revising, I realized, is like weeding in its attempt to eliminate the extraneous. The arrival of a new growing season has similarities to beginning another draft of a book. Plants, moreover, may be difficult to place at first, but finally, like sentences and words and paragraphs, their placement seems right.

Waiting is important both in the garden and while writing: a gardener waits for a border to bloom, the way a writer waits for memories or images or insights to come to mind. I remembered the many times I had patted wet soil around a green sprig, waited a few days for it to put forth leaflets, and then watched it double and triple in size within weeks. It made me understand that the power of photosynthesis was like the probability that the psyche's creative energy will provide ideas when writing. It was, of course, what Emily Dickinson and Edith Wharton had implied when they likened their creative imaginations to their flower gardens. After assuming that gardens grow by themselves, while books never do, I realized that I was not entirely on my own at my desk.

I also discovered that differences between gardening and writing are complementary, even essential, as one exercises the brain and the other the body. Working outside at the end of the day allowed my mind to rest, while writing in the morning allowed my cuts, bruises, and muscles to heal. I remembered on a trip to Japan my fascination with a bald monk outside a Buddhist temple plucking away with a pair of tweezers at moss under an ancient twisted tree; when I walked by him an hour later, he was still patiently bending over the velvety green patch, his mind undoubtedly far away. As the rhythm of weeding and deadheading puts my mind into a more relaxed state, between the overdrive of writing and the amnesia of sleep, the afternoon mindlessness restores mindfulness by morning. So while the garden steals time from writing, it gives it back in other ways. It supplies silent hours for new words to well up and for those already written to arrange themselves in different ways. And if writing is not exactly enjoyable, it is satisfying and gives meaning to living. It is unnecessary, I realize, to ask if art should serve life or vice versa, because they serve each other.

six

SHADOWS

————◆•◀ ▶•◆————

Need to take meticulous
care of myself these dark,
difficult days.

December 12, 1987

A N IMAGE LINGERS IN MY
mind of a blurry reproduction of a drawing on a postcard
showing an orchard infused with a
rosy glow. A girl named Clarissa
Deming, a pupil at a female academy in Litchfield, had drawn it almost two centuries ago. It seemed
remarkable the way she had placed
fruit trees in ten precise rows spaced
evenly apart, then neatly numbered
and named each of seventy varieties
of apples below. It all looked so perfect, and it reminded me of the
order I was trying to bring to my
garden as well as to the rest of my

life. In the picture all the trees have tiny upright trunks and rounded crowns without apples, as if it was high summer. When I later examined the original picture, I saw that the schoolgirl had first worked lightly in pencil on a plain piece of paper before drawing the trunks in ink with a quill pen and portraying the foliage with watercolor and brush. There was also the outline of a windowless barn and the straight line of a fence that protected the sweet fruit, bark, and twigs of the small trees from the teeth of tame and wild animals. I was attracted to this charming ink-and-brush illustration because it seemed all serenity and orderliness, but I would discover that my impression was an illusion.

When the drawing was done, around 1810, the orchard was evidently impressive. Clarissa's father, I learned, was a wealthy Litchfield merchant who collected many varieties of seeds and seedlings. Many of the apples in the orchard originated in Connecticut, while the tart Rhode Island Greenings came from my native state. At first I had only a vague sense of what the drawing meant to me, and I wondered what it might have signified to the teenage Clarissa. Did it allude to the idyllic Garden of Eden and its apple tree's promise of knowledge? Was it a way to please her father? Did it indicate a young girl's love for the natural world? Or did it, as I suspected, simply suggest a budding artist's desire to arrange and beautify what was around her? The portrayal of the family's orchard continued to intrigue me, and gradually I began to understand why: it looked like a young girl's vision of the benevolence and the

FOUR TENTHS of an ACRE

reasonableness of nature and, by implication, of human nature as well.

The image of Clarissa's drawing on the postcard aroused my off-and-on-again urge to plant a decorous orchard in my backyard, perhaps in a pattern like the one in her picture or in two long rows down the length of the lawn. It also reminded me that, until recently, Sharon had many orchards. Early on, almost every homestead had apple trees, and by the nineteenth century more than eighty different kinds of apples ripened every month of the growing season in New England. The sugary fruit was then pressed into cider or stored in barrels in dirt cellars during the long winters. By the middle of the twentieth century, however, as roads were paved and the hills of northwestern Connecticut became less isolated, apple blights and borers invaded the orchards, and the trees bore less abundantly. Yields could be increased by spraying, but the necessity of using poisons made me hesitant about planting the trees. Even so, I love seeing twisted and bent branches of old apple trees around town adorned with delicate displays of pale pink blossoms in spring before they bring forth their buggy fruit.

When I went to the Litchfield Historical Society's library to examine Clarissa Deming's actual drawing, I found imperfections that were invisible on the postcard. The schoolgirl's handwriting, illegible on the reproduction, labeled some trees with question marks and identified others as "vacant" or missing. It appeared that where cultivars had died or their names had been forgotten, the girl put images in anyway for the sake of perfect order. And while the reproduction's hue is pinkish, the original is tan, but even that tone is deceptive. The curator told me that Clarissa had most likely used black ink on white paper, but over the centuries the black had faded to brown, while the white had darkened. And although I had assumed that it was an apple orchard, four of the five trees at the ends of a few rows were classified as pears and peaches. I also discovered that Clarissa's drawing was not as inventive as I had first imagined. It was undoubtedly influenced by almost identical illustrations of deciduous trees and evergreens in a book titled *The Planter's Guide,* published in England in 1779, the kind that her father would have had in his library. The only difference between the pictures is that the trees in the book throw shadows while hers do not.

So her enchanting orchard was mostly an invented garden of trees. And her youthful vision of the predictability or perfectibility of existence had probably not been fulfilled by the time of her untimely death at the age of forty-two, virtually my age when I began another phase of life in the country. So my first impression of *Family Orchard,* as the drawing is called, did not prepare me for problems I had with trees on my land or, for that matter, difficulties with matters of the heart that I encountered after moving to Connecticut. My disillusionment in the museum that day, in fact, reminded me of my struggles for stability and harmony, as well as for compatibility, that were going on in my love life.

WHILE I LONGED FOR STEADINESS IN MATTERS OF THE heart, I vowed never to be made miserable again by any kind of dominating devotion or, for that matter, any other brand of difficult love. A man who came to see me after I moved to Sharon was also a writer, and our highly charged bond was usually accompanied by easy companionship. He had a very small apartment in Manhattan, so we spent most of our time together in Connecticut. Feeling emotionally enriched by living in the country made me doubt my desire to get married again; I liked being alone more than before, and I knew it was better for me as a writer. My immediate impression of this New Yorker with burning dark eyes had been his alternately humorous and gloomy, warmhearted or defeatist, nature. I was increasingly worried that the romance would not work out. My apprehension was underscored one day when walking toward bursts of red and yellow foliage around a high green meadow, and I felt a flash of exhilaration at the possibility of moving through life by myself. After becoming disappointed in him again for one reason or another, I broke off our increasingly painful relationship.

A few days later, I looked out the window and saw him standing on the green with red roses in hand. Irritated yet bemused, I invited him inside. When he asked me to marry him, I didn't say yes, but I didn't say no, either. It was a warm, sunny

spring day, and we went out into the backyard together. Crocuses were blooming among the windblown piles of brown
leaves, and heavy green heads of daffodils showed slits of
bright yellow. Little mounds of fresh greenery around the
bulbs seemed to be enlarging as we watched. I went into the
dark recesses of the barn for rakes so that we could remove
dead leaves from the delicate new growth. We raked and
talked, and he admitted that it had troubled him that the house
and yard were mine, not ours, but he was getting over it. Back
inside I asked him to open a stuck window, and as he did so
there was a loud crash as the glass shattered and he cut his
hand. I wiped up the blood and then drove him to the hospital
for stitches, believing the mishap was a bad omen. Nevertheless, I tried to be hopeful about eventually being able to tell
him yes.

When he returned the following weekends, we would go
into the garden again. We worked together in the dappled
light of the overhanging branches of the maple, where the
yellowish green florets had become small leaflets. Where I
wanted a flower bed alongside a fence, we dug up a small
white pine and planted it in the back of the yard; we also
moved arborvitaes that were too close to the house. He pushed
the heavy, noisy lawn mower over the large lawn, while I followed behind raking warm, moist, sweet-smelling grass clippings into piles, putting them into baskets, and carrying them
to the compost pile. I liked this man looking strong, tanned,
and smelling slightly of sweat, and I wanted the outdoors to

give him what it was giving me. When I met his train every week, he was exhausted and dispirited by his job in the city, but after a few days in the country, he seemed to regain his vitality. And when we worked together in the backyard—raking, weeding, watering, edging, staking, seeding, dead-heading, planting, and all the rest—I felt a sense of rightness about our relationship that I had rarely felt before.

At times he talked so ardently about the arboreal nature of trees—the stability of deep roots, the strength of mighty trunks, the aspirations of lofty branches—that it almost sounded like he wanted to be one himself. He admired the big Norway maple near the house, the one that was difficult to plant under. I loved its leafy greenness, too, which was so dense when I looked up into it that I could not see the sky. Its low branches were heavy and pendulous, and I liked to reach up and pull down a thick cluster of glistening green leaves around my head. At first its large, dark, moving shadow did not matter, and when someone suggested that I cut off lower branches to let in more light underneath, I dismissed the idea.

I apparently imagined that we were engaging in some version of a male and female agrarian partnership going all the way back to Adam and Eve. While I was glad to be in the garden by myself, being outside together had an element of eroticism to it. I was grateful for his strength and speed as he mowed, dug, and took out heavy stones from the ground, and he was glad to show them to me. Everything took longer when I did it alone because, besides having less muscularity, I liked to pull every last weed and cut every spent flower in a border before moving on to the next. Admittedly, we also worked well in the yard together because he knew little about gardening and was willing to take suggestions.

I wanted to believe that this man was a "green world lover," in the words of the feminist scholar Annis Pratt, meaning the gentle archetypal male in old myths and ancient illustrations with vines and leaves for a beard and hair. Or, a little more realistically, I hoped that he was a natural kind of man, spontaneous yet steady, whose love would be nourishing. What I did not realize is that this mythical green man sometimes embodies reckless Dionysian qualities that make him an exciting lover but an irresponsible husband. In *Archetypal Patterns in Women's Fiction,* Professor Pratt warns that in novels written by women, liaisons with these kinds of males usually end badly. Unaware of this but longing for a loving relationship, I hoped that our hours together in the garden would strengthen what was good between us and let the rest fall away.

After the garden beds were mulched in June, we hiked up a nearby mountain to see the masses of wild laurel bushes in bloom. We brushed by their shining leaves and pale blossoms on the narrow trail, as pinkish-white petals fell all over our hair and T-shirts, making me like a bride again, anointed for happiness. We agreed to get married, but then our resolve faltered. Nonetheless, I did not want to be swayed by my misgivings and give up on the possibility of love, even though one night I had a vivid dream about marrying the wrong person in the full regalia of a white wedding gown and veil. Instead, I hoped that matrimony would be a way to capture our love and make it last. I began planning a wedding for the June solstice, the longest and lightest day of the year.

In wedding pictures our tanned and glowing faces are highlighted by our pale ivory finery of linen, silk, and lace. Afterward we did more work in the backyard together. We took up struggling sod under the maple and put down compost for a shade garden of ferns, hostas, white bleeding heart, lily of the valley, and European wild ginger, a low-growing ground cover with glossy round leaves that tolerates dryness and deep shade. It was where Fred McGourty had warned me to fertilize frequently and mulch deeply to preserve nutrients and moisture if I wanted anything to grow, let alone bloom. Elsewhere in the yard, tall white trumpet lilies, purplish black hollyhocks, and the lacy lavender meadow rues dwarfed us by midsummer. In autumn we extended a flower bed beyond the shadow cast by the fence and enlarged the sunny bed by the barn, removing rocks and overturning wheelbarrows of dark, rich earth into it. In those euphoric months, my new husband used to hold me tightly in his arms at night and tell me that he was more in love than ever.

We had talked about turning the loft of the barn into a writing room for him, and after we set a wedding date, we started to plan the renovation of the old building. At one time the barn had held stalls for horses, and it still had a dirt floor and a horse trough with hay. As the work got under way, I planted bulbs in the back of the yard, where he would be able to see them in bloom from the loft's half-moon window. When we learned that the back wall had to be rebuilt, I decided to have sliding glass doors put where I kept garden tools, so the area would be flooded with strong western light in the afternoons. All the barn would lack was water, but I planned to bring in full watering cans when potting. After the construction was completed in late winter, we began to paint. I found it joyous working on the new spaces together, but I was eager to be done by the time the snow melted and gardening could begin.

After we finished the work on the barn, he became inexplicably moody and easily enraged; periods of blackness alternated with unpredictable bursts of affection. When I asked him what was wrong, he was unable or unwilling to say, only that he had to reach bottom before he would get better again. Spring had touched the garden with green, and it was only in the garden that I could banish troubling thoughts. (Persephone, I reluctantly remembered, was picking flowers when Hades took her to the underworld and fed her a pomegranate seed, an aphrodisiacal ambrosia that entrapped her during the darkest time of year.) When he told me that he was going to a writer's colony for six weeks instead of using his new room in the barn, I became upset. In his absence, the empty loft was like a rejection of our life together, especially after all our effort and expense. I learned how to start the lawn mower and threw myself into spring gardening, sometimes staying outside all day. Behind the barn I took up grass and put down wood chips for a work area near the compost piles, then covered the building's foundation with raised beds made from heavy hand-hewn beams removed during the renovation. On rainy days I searched in junk shops for barrels, baskets, and trunks to hold garden tools.

When my husband returned, he was in a better state of mind. On a long walk together, he vowed to give more to his writing and to our marriage. Our harmony lasted while the bearded iris and then the peonies bloomed, long enough for us to celebrate our first wedding anniversary. A few months later he was, in my eyes, acting erratically again. He decided to leave his job in New York and do more writing in Sharon, and I worried about who he would be: the loving or the angry man. As his mood darkened, he tried to draw me into it, but I resisted; I wanted him to feel better instead of feeling worse myself. Sometimes he blamed his mood on what he called his demons, but other times he blamed me. One day he suddenly suggested that I sell the house and move with him to Ireland, where it might be easier for him to write. I was appalled that he would even ask. That winter it was comforting to go into the barn by myself, light a fire in the little woodstove, sweep up spilled soil and brush away cobwebs, oil and sharpen my tools. Or I would pull on my boots and go out in the snowy yard to chop away at the overgrown rose of Sharon bushes with large ratchet clippers.

By spring we were arguing about whether to trap the woodchucks that lived nearby under a neighbor's barn. They devoured the daylilies at the far end of the yard, then moved nearer the house to munch on the phlox, delphiniums, and my other prized perennials. While I was devastated by the damage, my husband seemed strangely attached to the destructive beasts. I was also afraid that they would attack my cocker spaniel: when she ran up to them with her tail wagging, they hissed and bared their teeth, stopping her in her tracks but not scaring her away. For a while I tried blocking the woodchuck holes with rocks. Then I went ahead and bought a Have-a-Heart trap, baited the steel contraption with a carrot, and set the hair-trigger mechanism. The next morning I found a frightened woodchuck inside, then drove it into the woods and let it go near a brook. As our second wedding anniversary approached, I said to my husband that at least we were still married, then immediately regretted the remark.

The following spring I was waiting as usual for the ground to thaw and the air to get warm, but, unlike other years, I was not looking forward to gardening. *"Waiting to begin to garden. Somehow not—yet—as exhilarated about it as in other years, even though this year I'll have more time for it,"* I wrote in my garden notebook. I had finally faced the fact that my husband had become envious of the garden, and I dreaded his reaction when I went into the yard. He complained that I paid more attention to the flowers than to him and this, he admitted, made him feel unimportant. To get me to notice him, he said sarcastically, he would have to dress up like a peony. (If I dominated him the way I ruled over a peony, I thought, I would be a dominatrix.) And, he added, if I gave to him what I gave to the garden, he would be more successful as a writer. I was incredulous because we had had so much happiness together outside, or at least I thought we had. I had assumed that if he was given air and light and space like, well, a plant, he would flourish, but evidently I was wrong.

His angry words had their effect, and I did less and less gardening. For a while I wondered if I *was* neglecting my husband while gardening and writing a book; admittedly, it was difficult being both a writer and a wife because when writing I had to turn my attention inward toward my work instead of outward toward him. *"It's terrifying to feel so black—to feel one's inner resources aren't enough—do not buoy or heal,"* I wrote then. *"I don't remember any more difficult time. Many weeks of low-key depression and four a.m. wakefulness about how to relieve the various stresses and feel nourished."* Meanwhile his litany of complaints about me and my garden was a reminder of Simone de Beauvoir's theory about woman being to man what nature is to woman. I agreed. It seemed that females were often more empathic toward males than males were toward them, so they tended to turn to nature for nurturing instead. Certainly my garden gave dependable pleasure, while my marriage did not. It also made fewer demands than my husband; it was there to be seen, but it did not demand admiration.

Eventually his accusations about my being happier in the garden than with him became a self-fulfilling prophecy, and I escaped into the backyard as often as possible. *"Ricocheting between life's blows and the healing quality of the garden,"* I noted. The laws of nature seemed more rational than those of our relationship. My efforts outside rewarded me more reliably. On days when the marriage felt particularly precarious, it was reassuring to feel the firmness of my own land under my feet. It was also where I knew, more or less, what to expect: I could predict when the daffodils would bloom, that the bleeding hearts would follow, and then the irises, peonies, roses, clematises, lilies, hostas, asters, chrysanthemums, and all the other perennials would flower in their turns. As time went on, I came to the conclusion that gardening, instead of depriving my husband of my attention, was what enabled me to give him anything at all. If I could just get out the basement door and go through the motions of deadheading or weeding, while my dog moved from shadow to shadow at my side, I would gradually feel better. On days when my despondency made it difficult to pick up a rake, I tried to remember this. Still disheartened a few weeks before our third anniversary, I took off my wedding ring, and then he took his off, too.

ALONG WITH APPLE ORCHARDS, NEW ENGLANDERS HAVE always adored elms. The earliest settlers saw *Ulmus americana* in swamps, and they dug up its saplings and planted its seeds.

The shapely slender trunk, they discovered, was a hardwood that rooted easily and grew rapidly to more than a hundred feet. They believed it to be enduring: branches tended to bend rather than break in high winds; it tolerated exposure to wood smoke and, remarkably for a species found in wetlands, dry summers. What came to be regarded as the queen of American trees also had an elegant air as its lofty branches rose heavenward before gracefully sweeping down. After a visit to Connecticut, Thoreau suggested that the tree inspired elevated emotions, observing that "such an avenue of elms as that of Sharon is itself a poem and a picture, surviving to remind us of what has been and may yet be again." The number of elms in a town, he went on, "is a measure of its civility."

Village improvement societies in the nineteenth century encouraged townspeople to place elms along village streets. A straight row of young elms was planted on each side of Sharon's elongated green, a third row went on the opposite side of Main Street, and a fourth went across Upper Main Street. The driving force behind the plantings was a man who lived in an old family home on Upper Main with a nursery— possibly planted with elm seedlings—out back, according to an old map. Maybe he was motivated because the countryside outside the village had been almost entirely deforested for farmland and firewood for the iron industry. By 1883, the saplings stood about six feet tall, according to grainy black-and-white images of the green taken on glass plates by an amateur photographer, George Marckres, who ran a variety store and soda fountain on Main Street. Before long an airy canopy of elm branches arched high over the green, giving the former grazing ground the appearance of a grassy park. By 1939, when the town celebrated its two-hundred-year anniversary under the leafy mantle of the sheltering elms, proud and patriotic speeches assumed that the nature of Sharon and the majesty of the elms were essentially the same.

By then, however, Dutch elm disease had already entered the United States in imported elm veneer on its way to furniture factories in the Midwest. The fungus carried by elm bark beetles spread swiftly because the elms were planted so close together. Men hired by the state identified infected trees with telltale withering and browning leaves and ordered them chopped down and burned. The epidemic was slowed, but after conservation efforts ended during World War II, the beetle became widespread and killed millions of trees across the country. Most of Sharon's elms were incinerated in enormous pyres, leaving little more than electricity poles on the green. The loss of their lovely and protective presence was devastating, as old-timers tell it. "That's nature," retired Sharon tree warden Bob Carberry remarked sadly, who had cut down many of the hardwoods with hand tools in the 1940s and 1950s.

In the 1960s, another town beautification group raised money to buy locusts and shadblows to plant among the remaining sugar maples and ashes. When I moved to town twenty years later, a few surviving elms stood in an uneven line along the green. I can, in fact, watch from my desk as leaves on a low branch turn pale green in April and bright yellow in October; I am glad, however, that I cannot easily see the side of the tree that is sheared to make space for a utility pole and its tangle of heavy wires. In recent years the Sharon Green Preservation Association has hired an arborist to inoculate the elms and to plant disease-resistant ones along with a wide variety of other trees. It is impossible to line them up in orderly rows anymore because of underground sewer and water lines, so now they are arranged naturalistically, giving the green a more informal look.

One afternoon I asked at a nearby nursery about pruning perennials, and the extroverted Englishwoman who worked there told me, "When in doubt, cut back!" Around the same time my mother started to teach me how to trim trees and bushes to make them shapelier. She had mastered the intricacies of pruning as well as espalier and topiary; around her home in Rhode Island, evergreens were clipped into spirals and one was the shape of an enormous chicken. I was a willing student because I, too, favored sunny areas over shady ones, efflorescence over greenery. One of the tools she gave me was an extremely sharp, ragged-toothed Japanese handsaw that easily severed large limbs. As I watched my mother and listened to her, I gradually became bolder about sawing off big branches that, once amputated, could not, of course, be reattached. It was easy to cut down the languishing white pine that my husband and I had transplanted but harder to know what to do about low branches of the large maple.

I wanted to eliminate higher limbs than those reached by ladder, so I used a pruning pole. When even it would not go far enough, I telephoned an arborist. At first I asked him to take off an offending bough here and there, like those in the mulberry tree (probably from Sharon's silk-making days in the nineteenth century) that splattered ripe, black berries all over the driveway in June. Removing brush, branches, and small trees along the edge of woods behind the barn had revealed *"the beauty of the great trees,"* I marveled in my notebook. Then three years after marrying, I took the momentous step of having entire trees taken down. First to go was a dying white ash, whose leafless limbs grasped at the sky like a bony claw. Along with other ashes, it was under attack from a fungus that, like Dutch elm disease, prevents sap moving from roots up to leaves. Another tree that bothered me was a deformed elm overhanging the barn. After I had put compost piles near its trunk, nutrients touched off a rapid growth spurt; one limb in particular began to grow vigorously toward the light, arching over the building to shade the heliotropic plants in the sun bed, and even entangling branches of the silver maple all the way across the yard.

Despite favoring flowers over trees, I found it difficult to destroy an arboreal presence, so I usually had it done in winter, when the tree was leafless and seemed less of a living being. As the cutting began, the scream of the power saw sounded to me like the agony of a dying animal, so I would retreat inside and try not to listen. When I confessed this to the arborist, Mike

Root, he admitted that what he liked best about his work was climbing into a tree before turning on his saw. In those quiet minutes he watched and listened for birds, while he looked around and imagined what the town was like when the two-hundred-year-old trees were young.

I liked the small silver maple in the yard with slender, silvery green leaves that whirled in the wind and turned soft yellow in the fall. After the brittle wood of its trunk split down the middle like a wishbone from the weight of snow on leaves during a freak October snowstorm, I had it wired back together again. A few years later, the pretty tree had grown so rapidly that its shallow enmeshed roots formed an impenetrable mass where it was impossible to plant. Meanwhile, the roots aggressively probed beds all around the garden. Its spreading foliage also cast too much shade on the sun beds, so one February I had Mike dismember it for me. I watched from a window with conflicted feelings, while the large grayish tangle of dying twigs and branches was piled up on the snow.

My mother had shocked me by suggesting that I cut down my beloved Norway maple, an invasive species that drops multitudes of winged seedpods, and plant a rarer flowering tree instead. I rejected the idea, but I finally did ask Mike one winter to remove a few low branches to give the bleeding heart, primroses, jack-in-the-pulpits, and other shade plants underneath it more light. *"It's above freezing and the poor maple is dripping sap,"* I observed at the time. *"I hope not too much damage is done, but it's a good time to do it—the last gasp of winter—and the men walked on snow and did not do damage by walking on plants."* Afterward I worried that the tree was weakened because its crown did not seem as magnificent as before, but Mike reassured me that it naturally let in more light than most maples.

As I look back, I wonder what my husband went through, a man with so much admiration for trees, as many of them around the yard were demolished. Oddly enough, I do not recall any protest from him, or even if he was present when one or another came down. (My garden notes reveal that he did move and stack the wood of the ash after its demise.) All I remember is our increasing misery together. A month or so after the deformed elm and dying ash were taken down, I did what I had long been thinking about: I told him to stay in the city and not come to Sharon anymore.

That spring, as days got longer and lighter, my eagerness to garden gradually returned. *"Very thrilled to be able to pour my energy into this work. Desperately need it,"* I wrote. *"Imagine the garden will be very lovingly caressed this spring!"* I cut and raked the lawn by myself but forgot to raise the mower blade, so the grass was shorter than it was supposed to be. With more energy as well as time to myself, I was able to edge around the entire yard in a matter of weeks. At moments I felt flashes of well-being that promised to diffuse my heartache. On our fourth wedding anniversary, my husband sent me red roses along with letters expressing love and anger, all intertwined. Even though I was able to destroy trees that cast too much shadow, I was unable to be that ruthless with him. When I talked to him on the telephone, I was touched by his tenderness and let him return. We did a little gardening together again that summer, but I remained wary because I did not expect our marriage to last.

Ideally, the canopy of a tree is sheltering, the way the big maple shields my home from the west wind and hot summer sun. But some trees are lethal, I later learned from a nurseryman planting magnolias in the yard, who pointed out a poisonous black walnut right over the fence in the woods. Farmers have known for centuries that the native *Juglans nigra* is a danger to crops like potatoes and alfalfa as well as to apple trees. The tree sickens or kills when nearby roots happen to draw up its toxin; even remaining bits of its roots in the ground can cause necrosis. Some ornamental shrubs are vulnerable, and I worried that magnolias might be susceptible, too. Perhaps the black walnut's presence had already done damage, since I had tossed its leaves and nuts into the compost for years. Walnut is used for making fine furniture and musical instruments, so I unsuccessfully tried to give the wood away and regretfully had it cut up for firewood.

When my husband's state of mind darkened again, and I found myself weeping on Christmas Eve, I knew the marriage was over at last. Six years earlier I had moved to the country with high hopes, but the troubled relationship was now undermining my new life. I remembered that Georgia O'Keeffe, a Wisconsin farmer's daughter, had likened herself to "a plot of warm moist well tilled earth with the sun shining on it" in a letter to a man she was leaving. I looked up the passage in my biography about her and read the rest of the words she had written: "It seems I would rather feel starkly empty than let any thing be planted that can not be tended to the fullest possibility of its growth. . . . I do know that the demands of my plot of earth are relentless if anything is to be grown on it—worthy of its quality. . . . If the past year or two or three has taught me anything it is that my plot of earth must be tended with absurd care—By myself first—and if second by someone else it must be with absolute trust. . . . It seems it would be very difficult for me to live if it were wrecked again just now." *"So I must tend my garden very carefully,"* I noted in my journal that day. Like O'Keeffe, I realized that I had to safeguard myself against a disruptive and dangerous love.

On a June afternoon near the time of our fifth wedding anniversary, my husband arrived at the house to pick up some possessions. Lengthening shadows had softened the strong light in the garden, and I was contentedly digging holes in enriched dirt and planting little bushes in them. When I saw him, I remembered the tale of the mythological maiden who banishes the male who interferes with her relationship with nature. By then I knew that it is sometimes necessary to leave a person you love, and I turned down his invitation to leave the garden for a little while. A year later a judge in the small stone courthouse in Litchfield banged down her gavel and declared us divorced. Afterward, I had a dream about discovering a new room; it gave me the same sense of elation and expansion as after renovating the barn, but I was unsure what to do with the unexpected space. When I woke up, I remembered the empty writing room upstairs in the barn with its view of tree branches in the woods. But it is a hideaway I rarely use, because it has an old trunk filled with love letters.

My version of this marriage differs from the story of Adam and Eve in the "garden eastward in Eden." The original garden had every tree that was beautiful and bore fruit, including trees of life and of the knowledge of good and evil. The latter had a delectable but forbidden fruit, as everyone knows, and when a serpent tempted the woman with obtaining wisdom, she took a bite of an apple and passed it on to the man. Then God, in the ancient account, angrily banished his naked creatures from the paradisiacal garden before they could taste the fruit of the tree that promised everlasting life. This expulsion has always seemed to me extreme punishment for curiosity and willingness to take a chance. In any event, after another woman banished a man from a small and imperfect garden in Connecticut, she had a little more wisdom and her garden had much less shadow.

seven

WEATHER

———◆◄ ►◆———

Came back from four days
away to a disheartening
mess. Violent rains had
washed most of the mulch
from the beds and
broken many plants.
A bird's nest was even
washed out of a tree.

May 23, 1988

I THOUGHT I KNEW THE
weather of New England well,
but it is another matter to know it
as a gardener. In northwestern
Connecticut, rivers wind through
valleys and hills that rise more than
two thousand feet above sea level,
a difference in altitude that creates
dramatic atmospheric contrasts in
the sixty-three-square-mile township of Sharon. On days when the
thermometer hovers near freezing
at seven hundred feet in the village,
the soft rain on Main Street is likely
to be dangerous black ice three
miles away in the higher hamlet of

Ellsworth. Even on my half acre, the temperature is always much warmer near the south side of the white barn than in the shadow of the fence a few feet away.

Along with variability, there is little predictability in the weather that passes through the countryside. Convulsions of wind, snow, and rain constantly roil over the region, caused by collisions of northern winds, southern breezes, and gusts moving in from the sea. These moods of nature continually change from season to season and even from hour to hour. A few hot days in March may be followed by bitter nights in May, although scorching summers are becoming more common than the raging winter blizzards of the past. Environmentalists expect global warming to make the climate even more erratic, violent, and extreme. Growing anything in my garden, where the days between frosts last for about four months, is, needless to say, a challenge.

I like to take photographs of the garden at its best, but there are only six or seven days, usually in June, during the 125 or so days of the growing season when I want to reach for my camera. One August I wrote in my garden notebook that the flower beds were battered by *"too much drought, too much heat, too much rain, too much wind."* Violent thunderstorms had flattened tall lilies and rotted dahlia petals, while hot light had turned the leaves of the purplish black hollyhocks into lacy shadows of themselves. As always, the heart of the garden alongside the barn looked terribly thin.

Where the eye wanted green, the barn's bright whiteness

blanched blossoms and desiccated leaves. I asked myself if I should have planted evergreens there after all, as Fred McGourty had once suggested, instead of flowers. I fantasized about painting the building the traditional dull red of a New England barn. A muted maroon backdrop might bring out and complement the pinks and blues and even the greens. Yet when it was time to paint the barn again, I lost my nerve and again went for the usual white. Next time, I vow, I will paint the wall behind the flower bed the same dark green as the doors and shutters of the house.

At first the border beside the barn was too shady, but then it became too sunny after I had the overhanging branch of the elm cut down. Afterward the sun radiated off the chalky clapboards hour after hour, intensifying the midsummer heat to well over a hundred degrees on August afternoons. On January nights the temperature drops to as low as fifteen to twenty degrees below zero. But in winter, even after I shaded the foot or so of ground beneath the overhanging barn roof with straw, leaves, or pine branches, the glare of the weak winter sun allows alternating thaws and freezes to push roots out of the ground.

While hard frosts flatten herbaceous plants every autumn, summer heat destroys more insidiously. The American Horticultural Society, which has started to record high temperatures as the planet heats up, tells me that my garden can expect two weeks to a month of days when it is hotter than eighty-six degrees. (Their calculation, of course, does not take into consideration the waves of heat reflecting off the south wall of the barn.) During those hot hours, heat pulls moisture from the living tissues of leaves, leaving them juiceless before burning them and turning them brown. Stately blue delphiniums grow beautifully in May, and then collapse when it heats up in July, leaving a gaping hole in the border. Even the eager little forget-me-nots turn black and as brittle as brushes. Meanwhile, I watch worriedly while buggy leaves of plants in the border by the barn go limp in the afternoon and hope that they will revive when shadows later fall over them.

So many losses had happened in this border that I began to wonder if it was cursed. Suspecting that there was something wrong with the soil—maybe I had not removed enough packed ash from the old driveway underneath the topsoil—I took a desperate step. With the help of a handyman, I dug up every plant, shoveled out all the dirt, then put in compost and manure mixed with the old soil before planting everything again. To my dismay, in the following years the perennials still did not flourish and the border continued to look sparse. *"Garden disappointing, not full enough. It needs more bushy green foliage. Looks spindly. Will maturity do it?"* I asked in my journal, then hurried out to buy dianthus, lobelia, snapdragons, and baby's breath for fillers. *"Anything for a feeling of fullness this year."* But I hated the unnatural way they looked, and a few weeks later wrote in disgust: *"Half-grown perennials and bright annuals in a row."* While the shady side of the garden was overflowing with astilbes, foxgloves, primroses, lamiums, and a few spears of irises, I noted that the *"sun bed is still awful with two rows like soldiers either side of the drip line of the roof."* I also wanted the heights of plants to be gradual, but they jumped from ten-foot meadow rue to four-foot phlox to inch-high ground covers. But because of the drip line, there was not enough depth to the bed for more plantings.

After failing to get tall perennials like delphiniums and hollyhocks to camouflage the stark whiteness of the building, I decided to nail trellises on the clapboards for climbing roses and clematises. They did well on trellises in partial shade, but those in full sun stayed bare most of the time. I tried mulching the ground to keep roots moist; pine bark chips gave way to shredded autumn leaves and the little locust leaves that fell in front of the house, but there were never enough; when I found quantities of finely ground mulch at a nearby nursery, I bought it by the truckload. Even so, I repeatedly lost a lovely "New Dawn" rose with a reputation for vigor. I researched other vines that might thrive on the side of the barn, but none promised to grow without ruining my color scheme or destroying the clapboards. I planted another "New Dawn," gambling on hope over experience, while vowing to give it more water, but it, too, has refused to grow up its trellis, and I do not understand why.

As daylight lessens after the June solstice, so do my hours in the garden; it is difficult to do strenuous work in the heat. Much of it is already done, with only deadheading and watering left. Some August days it seems as if the garden is overexposed as if by the unremitting glare of a flashbulb. Brilliant light, paradoxically, makes it more difficult to see, so on such days the flower beds appear to fade away before my eyes. In order to avoid the blinding light, I go outside at dawn, when the dewy greenery holds the last of the nighttime shadows. As long as the sun stays below the roofline, I rapidly clip and stake in the house's shade, racing against the upward rise of the hot orb. When an explosion of sunlight floods the garden and scorches the skin on my arms, I empty my basket and start toward the shrinking shadow near the house. As shadows creep back in late afternoon, I also return as pale flowers regain their hues in the softening light. Darkness arrives incrementally on long summer evenings, and only when I can no longer tell a weed from a flower do I reluctantly return inside.

A drought eliminates a growing season in Sharon every decade or so, but hot, dry spells of ten to twenty days happen all the time. Spring seems like an unstoppable force of nature, until lack of rain halts it in its tracks, turning daffodil buds into empty pouches. When flowers open in the fiery heat during a drought, they wilt within hours. While it refuses to rain, the days become a terrible, tense time of withholding. A dry spell is a more painful kind of torture than a violent storm, because it is impossible to know when it will finally end. As growth slows and then stops altogether, it seems difficult to breathe. In the presence of dying plants, I am reminded of a so-called life force that wears the kindly face of Mother Nature one day and the frightening face of Medea the next. Day after day of dryness is the only time when I want to turn my back on the garden, as it becomes overwhelmingly obvious that nature's ability to destroy is far greater than my ability to protect.

The garden often gets far less rain than the inch a week it requires, especially when temperatures soar into the nineties and stay there for days. So why not just water? I try to soak or shade anything newly planted, but it is impossible to quench the thirst of everything in the yard. I also try to hold off watering so perennials will develop deep roots because water restrictions are imposed in the village during droughts; I also dislike using costly and chlorinated town water more than necessary. When I cannot stand seeing vegetation suffer any longer, I finally get out the sprinkler or soaker hose. *"The garden seems very dry, so I watered, though I felt I might do more harm than good by not watering enough. Couldn't resist. The top inch is like dry powder,"* I noted. When a downpour finally breaks a summer drought, it feels like a state of grace. I like to look out a window while a wall of silvery water falls heavily off the barn roof into the border below, where it puddles for a few moments before being sucked into the ground. As the rainwater disappears, I imagine it rushing up from the roots to relieve depleted green tissues. In a matter of minutes and hours, wilted leaves miraculously fill out and buds begin to uncurl.

Usually, a summer rain arrives with violent gusts of wind that whip the greenery around, knock down flower stalks, and even rip tops off trees. One July afternoon, when friends and neighborhood children were visiting me, the sky suddenly darkened, as if a thunderstorm was approaching. The wind picked up, and the weathervane on the barn roof gyrated wildly in the electrified air. A purplish green mass of sinister clouds appeared in the west, flashing with lightning. It got preternaturally dark outside, and when the power went off, I lit candles while we waited apprehensively for the fury of the storm to pass. A little while later, the radio reported that a pair of tornadoes with winds of well over a hundred miles an hour had passed overhead, one right after another. In Sharon the twisters had only lifted the roof off a barn, but in other villages they snapped ancient pines in two and uprooted maples and left behind a horrifying scene of destruction, including injuries, a young girl's death, and millions of dollars in property damage.

The way nature gives with one hand and takes with the other is difficult to grasp. This is because we want, perhaps we need, the natural world to be more than amoral. In the essay "Against Nature," Joyce Carol Oates explains her resistance to the usual understanding of what she calls Nature as benevolent on the grounds that it lacks humor, morality, purpose, irony, meaning (and words!), all the while mocking the aspirations and ideals of humanity. Whatever it is that we call by the name nature, she writes, "eludes us even as it prepares to swallow us up, books and all." She states that those in the throes of biophilia, the love of nature, are in denial of reality about nature's terrible rages and sulks. I grudgingly accept her logic— the belief in nature as benign or bad, or, for that matter, having any meaning at all, is a matter of giving ourselves too much importance. While my mind agrees with her, however, the rest of me remains fervently in denial.

Meanwhile, I keep on denying and replacing dying plants, despite having witnessed tempestuous rages of nature since early childhood. During September hurricanes on the Rhode Island coast, I remember swirling, battering winds that whipped salt water inland to sear and tear apart vegetation in gardens and fields. Once, after a storm subsided, I went outside with my cousins who lived next door to try to stand upright against the weakening wall of moist air. As the fast-moving clouds pulled apart, the sun came out, all sparkling innocence, and illuminated the awful sight and acrid smell of decaying vegetation in the bright breeze, as if nature were mocking its own madness.

REFLECTING ON DAMAGE DONE BY DROUGHTS, BLIZZARDS, heat waves, black frosts, tornadoes, and other meteorological events, I asked myself how gardeners and farmers go on when at any moment everything they grow might be destroyed by the hand of nature. Attempting to understand how others have dealt with the vicissitudes of weather, I turned to old diaries and other documents in the Sharon Historical Society. Letters mention a snowstorm in the 1770s that left too much snow to travel by sleigh and horses, and Pastor Cotton Mather Smith and his son strapped on a pair of Indian snowshoes and set off for the long walk to New Haven, so the young man would not be late for classes at Yale. Townspeople remembered "the great white hurricane" of 1888 for a generation, when wind gusts blew snow into drifts as high as forty feet. All the diarists, whether from farm families or not, almost always began daily entries with a description of the day's weather. It also happens to be the way I begin an entry in my garden notebook.

In the summer of 1854, Sharon farmer George Woodward kept a diary that reads like an agrarian tragedy. After his land on West Woods Road started to green, he noted that the biggest snowstorm of the winter had buried his plow up to its handles. During June hoeing and haying, drought and heat dealt him another blow. On July 4 the temperature hit ninety-eight degrees in the shade, and "vegetation suffers much for want of rain," he wrote. Then a "dreadful" thunderstorm tore limbs off maple trees near his house. His pastures dried up and the trees looked like they were dying. "Hot and O dear how dry," the farmer lamented in August. "Mercury at 100 above 0." It was not until the middle of September, after the growing season was over, that an all-night rain finally soaked his farm.

The temperamental weather made me wonder how a farmer in Sharon was able to plan a day's work, let alone predict a season's harvest. A few pleasant days allowed George to gather his meager crops of corn and potatoes. For a while in October it was too hot to work outside, then the thermometer dropped below zero in November, forcing him to thresh oats in his bitter cold barn. After a heavy snowfall in early December, the temperature soared to seventy degrees the day after Christmas. "Soon lose the sleighing if this weather lasts," he noted laconically, as if fatalism were the only way to face the exasperating and enigmatic whims of the weather.

Weather is the wild card of everyday life, the topic all growers talk about. Edith Wharton wrote in her memoir about starting to garden in New England on a rocky half acre despite "the ruthless gales of the Rhode Island sea-coast." Her frustration with the moods of nature near the ocean was, in retrospect, nothing compared with what she suffered during summers in the inland hills of Massachusetts. In the spring of 1902, the Whartons arrived to spend their first April in Lenox, just in time for an assault of snow, hail, wind, and rain. Undaunted, or believing the awful weather was an aberration of nature, Edith went ahead with ambitious plans for a number of formal gardens—sunny, shady, rock, and vegetable—along the classical lines of harmony and proportion that she admired in Italy. Attempting to adapt to the more northern American climate, she used hardy evergreens, like arborvitaes and hemlocks, rather than tender southern European shrubbery, such as cypresses and camellias. She also had her heart set on the flowers that she assumed would do better in the wetter and cooler climate of New England.

The next spring, however, she was shocked at finding an "ugly burnt-up" landscape in Lenox, as she put it in a letter. "There has been an appalling drought of nine weeks or more, & never has this fresh showery country looked so unlike itself," she wrote in anguish to her friend Sally Norton a month later. "The dust is indescribable, the grass parched & brown, flowers & vegetables stunted, & still no promise of rain! You may fancy how our poor place looks, still in the rough, with all its bald patches emphasized." Everything had come to nothing, and she turned on her gardener, as if he could have stopped the will of nature, believing he had failed her because of "drink or some other demoralization." She ended her letter by saying, "I try to console myself by writing about Italian gardens instead of looking at my own."

The following summers had more reasonable weather, and Edith devoted herself to cultivating her prize-winning flowers—sweet peas, snapdragons, gladioli, poppies, phlox—most of which were started or grown by a gardener in her greenhouse. She ecstatically described her flower garden in another letter to her friend, exulting that with "intense blue Delphinium Chinense, the purple & white platycodons, etc.— really with the background of hollyhocks of every shade from pale rose to dark red, it looks, for a fleeting moment, like a garden in some civilized climate."

While the temper of the weather in the Berkshire Hills might have moderated for a while, the Wharton marriage was increasingly turbulent. Even though Edith regarded the Mount as her first real home, the scandal of her divorce in the years before World War I made it impossible for her to remain in America. After staying in Lenox for a mere eight or so summers until 1910, she moved to France and bought a villa with a garden ten miles north of Paris. She then recalled the Berkshires as a beautiful but harsh land; in "Gardening in France" she admitted that she had been glad to say good-bye to "the late frosts and burning suns" of her native country. When she looked back at her attempts to garden in New England, she recalled "the mowing-down in a night of painfully nursed 'colour-effects,' and [returning] in the spring to the blackened corpses of carefully sheltered hemlock hedges and box-borders, [and learning] from cruel experience the uselessness of trying to 'protect' ivy, or to persuade even the tough ampelopsis to grow on sunny walls." She complacently concluded that: "to a gardener who has battled with such climates for twenty years, for the sake of a few brief weeks of feverish radiance, there is a foretaste of heaven in the long leisurely progression of the French summer."

In France she got an old fountain going, drainage put in, overgrown trees and hedges cut down, and manure spread over the seven acres. Then she began to garden again. "The mere fact that box, ivy, jasmine and climbing hybrid tea-roses belong to the fundamental make-up of the least favoured garden; that roses begin to bloom in June and go on till December; that nearly everything is 'remontant' and has plenty of time to flower twice over; this blessed sense of leisureliness and dependableness of the seasons of France, of the way the picture stays in its frame instead of dissolving like a fidgetty [*sic*] *tableau-vivant,* creates a sense of serenity in the mind inured to transiency and failure," she wrote. "My own translation into this horticultural heaven took place only two years ago, and already the New England gardening-wrinkles have been smoothed from my brow and my confidence in the essential reasonableness of Nature has been restored."

I read her words with envy, also willing to believe that the weather was better almost anywhere else. On a visit to London one spring, I noticed that it was sunny and rainy almost every day, sometimes at the same time, making weather forecasts meaningless but public gardens lush. When I returned to Sharon, I discovered that it had not rained once, while temperatures had risen into the nineties, so again the border beside the barn was full of dead flowers and plants. "The nature of gardening is not to have it all one's own way," Fred McGourty wrote in his book *The Perennial Gardener,* a big understatement, I thought. One time when I complained about the weather to a friend with a cottage garden high on a hillside outside the village, she replied that we are lucky *because* gardening is so difficult: we never get bored, and we can be prouder of our successes; changes in weather and seasons are exciting, she added, and we can rest in winter. This is the attitude of a gardener who will never give up (and who, incidentally, is very knowledgeable about Edith Wharton's gardens).

As I read more Wharton letters, I realized that Edith had been a bit overconfident. In the winter of 1920, cold winds and deep frosts decimated the semitropical garden of her winter villa on the Riviera. Still, she remained hopeful because, as she put it in early spring, "my bulbs are all sprouting, & this prodigal nature will repair things in a year." Gardeners, I realized, or at least those who persist, find ways to forget about the temper tantrums of nature. Even deliberate amnesia, however, and stubborn hope, could not prepare the author for what would happen nine years later, when, on her sixty-seventh birthday, in late January 1929, a storm destroyed the garden again.

Afterward, in early March, the weather capriciously got warmer than usual, but Edith felt as if the ligaments and limbs of her body were still intermingled with the lifeless roots and branches of her garden. In letters she described her "torture" over her "dead garden," and then she became dangerously ill. Her younger American friend Louis Bromfield, also a writer and gardener, observed that a drought was "a kind of illness from which she herself suffered physically, and the persistent cold rain which ruined the roses and damaged the prospects of a magnificent flowering was a kind of personal agony" because of her love for "the incalculable beauty which might be wrung from [the earth] by feeling and care and worship." The following October, as a true lady of the flowers, she resolutely set about planning yet another garden.

Edith Wharton and Louis Bromfield were fiercely competitive as writers, but as fellow gardeners they were extremely generous. "We seldom discussed our writing, but we talked frequently and at great length of our dahlias and petunias, our green peas and our lettuces," Louis remembered. One summer he took her to visit a prize-winning dahlia grower, Ludovic

Pierre Hureau, a communist "with bright blue eyes and fierce moustache," whom he described as a "strange, wild character, rather like something which had escaped from the forest into the village," in *Yrs. Ever Affly: Edith Wharton and Louis Bromfield.* Even though the lady and the "peasant," as Louis called him, had little in common, they walked around the acres of rare and beautiful blossoms like two old companions. Edith ordered an extravagant number of dahlia tubers that day, as if she had managed once more to forget about ruined gardens as well as her own frailty. The dahlia grower filled her automobile with bouquets of magnificent cut dahlias, and she drove away tired but happy. Sadly, she died the following August in 1937, before her new flowers bloomed.

NOTHING IS MORE STUNNING THAN THE SIGHT OF ICY branches glistening in the sunlight, after frozen rain has transformed familiar surroundings into a shimmering, silvery place. All goes well if the heat of the sun quickly melts the ice, but if it does not, the brittle, glassy beauty can suddenly shatter in a gust of wind, breaking branches and leaving behind a shocking scene of devastation. The icing of bushes and trees followed by disaster has happened many times in Sharon, when cracking boughs crash to the ground. Helen Smith, the great-granddaughter of Governor Smith, remembered her father waking her as a child one May morning at Weatherstone to see lilacs and other shrubs covered "branch, twig, and blossom with the sparkling diamonds of frost" right before a strong wind arose and smashed them to bits. Such experiences leave us with the task, once again, of trying to forget the dark side of nature, and wondering why Mother Nature plays cruel tricks on herself.

In early October a few years ago, the weight of wet snow on green leaves tore large limbs off trees and punctured the night with the sounds of loud explosions. *"Terrible snowstorm on Sunday,"* I noted. *"The green is devastated."* In winter, snow is beneficial because it keeps cold from deeply penetrating the ground and damaging roots. And in spring the pile of snow plowed off my driveway slowly melts into the growing border beside the barn. When there is not enough snow, like during a dreaded so-called green or brown winter, there can be trouble. Once, it was only a humorous trick; I was astonished one May when the buds of a climbing rose opened. What I had expected to be faintly pink blossoms nestled against a mass of dark green leaves were instead ugly, dark, purplish red roses. After looking back a few pages in my notebook, I realized what had happened: bitter cold during a snowless winter had killed the grafted rose above the ground, and the original root had grown back garish red. In the following days I clipped every last red flower off the large vine, until I had the chance to dig up the root-ball a few months later.

Reading over my notes reminds me of how many perennials I have lost. The list is long: white primroses and pink foxgloves, lupines, asters, malva, arabis, lovely scabiosa with its feathery violet flowers, and exuberant clematis vines full of buds and blossoms that were suddenly stricken with wilt at the height of their beauty. Most of the plants died for mysterious reasons. Some baked to death beside the barn, and others were killed by late frosts or overtaken by the ever-enlarging shadow of the maple. *"The white primroses I planted yesterday are in bad shock. There was ice on the bird bath this morning, so I will cover them with pots tonight,"* I wrote one spring. *"Black-eyed susans have survived. Doubtful about clematis. Two peonies so far. Trollius may be coming back. Delphiniums look promising."* Many of the disappearances were barely noticeable when the shoots failed to appear in the spring. Such quiet losses in the garden, I have discovered, are less distressing than those caused by violent weather. The longer I garden, the easier it is to regard a perennial vanishing here and another spreading there as nature's way of editing, a design, I admit, that is sometimes better than mine.

Losses in the garden, I also realize, are a reason to rely on resilient native species, like the black-eyed Susans (orangey golden flowers with round brown hearts that thrive in the hot, parched, poor soil along my driveway) that I plant as much by default as by desire. One spring I went to a nearby daylily farm and found a lovely miniature peach variety called "Little Tinker Bell." (Maddeningly, it and other daylilies clashed with the color of a nearby bush. *"The owner said that the day lilies were two weeks early because of the intense heat. Maybe next year the pink rhododendron and the yellow and orange day lilies will not bloom at the same time.*") It is reassuring that since the 1600s daylilies, grape hyacinths, daffodils, tulips, anemones, primroses, stars-of-Bethlehem, violets, columbines, irises, hollyhocks, roses, and delicate white or blue forget-me-nots have managed to bloom every year in New England gardens.

There are other ways to cope with the difficult climate as well as other challenges. A silvery green Russian sage with downy lavender flowers is unfazed by the hot light by the barn, so I took a cutting and propagated another to put there. I quarantine perennials that are overly aggressive, like loosestrife, to the cutting garden—eight mounds of earth separated by stone paths—in the back of the yard beyond the barn. It is also a place for herbs like basil and parsley, annuals like nasturtiums, extras like bearded iris, and disappointments like Oriental poppies that collapse in the middle of summer.

Species like peonies endure, even demand, bitter winters, as well as endless hours of sunlight, to bloom abundantly. Walking along Main Street one April, I had noticed fleshy pink tips poking out of the dirt in front of the Methodist parish house. As I watched them rise higher every day, they developed tops like unfurled green feathers, and then stalks that arranged themselves into shrubs, and finally produced shoots with plump round buds that opened into big blossoms in June. It was then that I recognized them as the herbaceous peonies my mother and grandmothers had grown in their gardens.

Even though I saw a rainstorm push the petals into the mud, I knew I had to have peonies in my garden.

The following autumn I placed three unprepossessing pieces of peony tubers barely under the soil in the bed near the barn. Their names were promising—"Charlie's White," "Miss America," and "Sweet Sixteen"—and the next fall I put in another three cultivars of a double pale pink named for Eleanor Roosevelt. After what Gertrude Jekyll called the plant's "dear rosy snouts" appeared the following spring, I carefully staked all the peonies, aware that their opulent blossoms would be too heavy for the stems, before they went into dignified repose for the rest of the season. Every year I wait for the peony week, when their blossoming is as dramatic as their disintegration, and when, after a few days, pale petals that feel like soft flesh loosen and fall lavishly on the ground. After a few seasons of increasingly bountiful blooms, my peonies began to go into decline; I was mystified, until I read about a fatal peony fungus. Even though the book said to destroy them, I dug them up, treated, divided, and replanted the healthiest roots. They regained their vigor, at least the ones named for Mrs. Roosevelt, which I regarded as a sign of the enduring qualities of a great lady as opposed to those of beauteous girls. Unfortunately, the briefly blooming plants did not ease the ongoing thinness of the border.

While nature often frustrates the gardener, I have never forgotten the warm spring day when a distinct edge of dark gray clouds appeared in the west. A wind arose and the temperature fell, and then snow began to swirl around the house. The day before I had been worried about keeping up with spring, but now spring had disappeared. Winter lasted only a day, however, until the other end of the nimbus appeared in the sky. When the late afternoon sun dropped below the edge of the cloud mass, a golden light gilded the snow and illuminated icicles dangling from rose vines, crystal caps on uncurled maple leaves, and white mounds over clumps of daffodils. I stared for a long time at the dramatic demarcation between the dark cloud mass and the pellucid sky, knowing that the snow would melt the next day.

And what is ordinary, yet also extraordinary, about spring in New England is the way it arrives so abruptly after winter. The contrast between the seasons cannot be greater, as colorlessness quickly is banished by an explosion of yellow and green growth. Every April it is the same: in early spring I go out the basement door feeling a little low and believing that I have no time for spring. Once outside and lifting fork loads of heavy, soggy leaves into the wheelbarrow and exposing pallid daffodil stalks to light, I begin to feel better. My memory of March is erased, and if I was not quite ready for all the work of spring, spring makes me ready for herself.

It is when I am feeling most horrified or disillusioned by existence that I turn to anarchic nature, refusing to believe that it is more ruinous than restorative. I suppose one can argue that the violent underbelly of nature enhances our appreciation of its life-giving aspect. I remind myself that every autumn the garden browns and blackens, and every spring it grows again. And that damage done by nature is often undone by nature itself. Tangling with nature is an ongoing lesson in resilience and recovery, I realize. It is impossible to take away the unpredictability of the weather or, for that matter, the uncertainty of life itself. I remembered that Joyce Carol Oates, after scorning those who only find beauty and inspiration in nature, ended her essay by asking, rhetorically, why not romanticize nature after all, "since it's there, common property, mute, can't talk back, allows us the possibility of transcending the human condition for a while . . . Why not." Why not?

eight

COLOR

———————

Finally some time to garden.
Cut back snow-in-summer,
malva, iris, etc. in garden
area. Gave little miniature
rose away and also pink
phlox. Little rose isn't hardy
enough for this climate and
phlox is the wrong color
next to the rose bush. Also
threw out plants in pots.

Not looking well.

August 25, 1992

ONE APRIL MORNING I HAD
been attempting to work on
the Louise Nevelson biography, trying to refine a passage about the
artist in her studio, while outside
my windows a glorious garden day
was unfolding. The sun was illuminating the greening world, where,
after a soft rainfall during the night,
the surge and swell of the bulbs and
buds was palpable. Forsythia bushes
were blasts of yellow, and the grass
had a tinge of green. Fluted creamy
double daffodils had been open for
a few days under a southern window, while behind the barn the pale

yellow tissues of others had just pushed out of their green sheaths. I felt infected, as if spring were a contagious condition, but I was trying to ignore what was happening on the other side of the glass and stay indoors.

My effort to keep my eyes away from the windows was a struggle because I was sure that the artist in my manuscript was enjoying making art more than I was enjoying writing about her. It didn't help when I remembered reading that all the arts except writing have sensory organs: painting has the eye, sculpture the hand, music the ear, singing the voice, and dance the body. Without a bodily instrument of its own, apart from the brain, the act of writing felt particularly painful to me that spring morning. Making art and tending plants seemed much more natural than expressing ideas and images through an intricate manipulation of black squiggles on white backgrounds. I stayed in my seat, but my body felt like a spring about to uncoil, a tension that was almost intolerable that morning.

Meanwhile I continued on, describing the way the sculptor moved around her studio, using her back and arms to heft and hammer old pieces of blackened wood. In warm weather, I remembered enviously, she made assemblages in her pseudo-garden behind her Manhattan brownstone, turning it into an outdoor extension of her studio. Artists often portray their workplaces as areas of possibility and pleasure; Henri Matisse in *The Red Studio,* for instance, drenches a rendering of his studio in passionate red paint as if it were life-giving blood. If I were to use words to describe my office, I would end up writing less about the muted colors inside than what I can see outside the windows on any given day: masses of tiny white flowers on candytuft bushes along the walkway in spring or deep pink crinkled blooms on rose of Sharon bushes by the end of summer.

Artists, of course, have always painted gardens. Claude Monet remarked that his real studio was the outdoors, and he would set up his easel in his garden to observe the changing prism of light throughout the day. "My first impression of it was of a space so filled with flowers that you could hardly put your hand between them; an artist's garden, not a horticulturist's," wrote Stephen Gwynn, author of *Claude Monet and His Garden: The Story of an Artist's Paradise,* after a visit to Giverny in the early 1930s, where Monet's daughter-in-law tended the garden the way the master had kept it. Artists' gardens are usually more naturalistic than horticulturalists' because most artists are more casual about them and like making art much more than weeding or pruning. To his neighbors' dismay, Monet manipulated his property to serve his painterly eye, once diverting a waterway to make the lily pond he immortalized in his work. The pond's reflections deliberately increased the luminescence of the light, as did his paving the road alongside the property to eliminate dust. What he wanted above all from his tangled mass of vegetation was "the flicker and brilliance of innumerable tiny points" of color and light, observed Gwynn.

My sister, who stopped designing others' gardens to paint, is less interested in creating what she calls "pictures" indoors and out than in creating images that evoke emotion. Like many artists, she wants to see the way plants grow naturally. She is also less fascinated by color (and thereby flowers) than form in gardens. What especially gets her attention is establishing "cool versus warm and dark versus light," she says. "I think of the size of a color—a large white lily versus tiny white baby's breath—and whether I want a recessive blue or an assertive warm color, rather than spending a lot of time fine-tuning colors and transitions à la Gertrude Jekyll." One reason she gave up working for others was that most of her clients wanted colorful gardens above all else.

Working in an achromatic art, like writing, makes color in the garden important to me. So it was interesting that Gertrude Jekyll attended art school in London in the 1860s with the intention of becoming a professional painter. It was when the ideas of the French chemist Michel-Eugène Chevreul—who created the color wheel as a way of establishing complementary chromatics—were in vogue. No shade stands alone, she learned, since its perception is changed by the vibrations of pigments around it: the presence of blue, for instance, intensifies pink. Like other young ladies of her day, she had studied botany, so when her eyesight weakened in adulthood, she was able to go from making art to designing gardens. By the 1880s, when she was in her forties, she was well known for her gardens. Along the principles of the color

wheel, she massed perennials in carefully graduated col-
orations, what she called "painting a landscape with living
things." Her rules about colors are a challenge to more casual
contemporary gardeners; certainly my garden is at times too
pink, too purple, too white, or too green even for me.

When I was very young, maybe six or seven, I took art
lessons from an artist who lived in a house perched on a steep
street in Providence. Gino Conti paved his courtyard with old
gravestones and in summer liked to sit and read in a patch of
tall weeds across the street. Classes were in his cellar, a dim
place with rough rock walls, and descending into it was like
entering a prehistoric cave; I would look up from a coarse sheet
of paper to see a gray rabbit inching across the floor or a large
turtle lurking near the warm stones of the huge hearth. At
home and school the emphasis was on rules, but in art class I
felt freer. Mr. Conti gave us bold primary colors—red, yellow,
and blue—and encouraged us to put our hands and brushes
into the watercolor pigments and do whatever we wanted on
the paper. He talked to us about what he called "beauty," so I
used to make bands of bright green grass and resplendent red
flowers under round yellow suns.

Why one form of expression takes hold and another does
not is a mystery to me. Around that time my mother took me
on weekly pilgrimages to the neighborhood library, a former
church that had become a large, airy, light-filled temple of
reading. There were more rules in the library than in art class,
but it did not matter to me. As I turned page after page of col-

orful children's books, I learned to decipher the meaning of the black words, and they eventually became more important to me than making pictures.

Green is a garden's background color, of course, and the foil for its flowers, but it is so ubiquitous a shade from grass to treetops that it is sometimes not seen at all. I often do not notice greenness, even the deep greens I prefer because of the way they flatter pale flowers. If a garden is to bloom during all the months of the growing season, it will always have large swaths of green—the plants that have gone by or are yet to flower. Part of the garden rests in a green state, while another, and then another, begins to bloom. Green, a blend of blue and yellow (as well as the shade of the sickening emotion of envy and the raw state of inexperience), is not, to my eye, the most appealing color in the prism. When my optic nerves record the sensation that my brain recognizes as green, it is not as pleasurable as, say, palish pink or as refreshing as white. This is peculiar since rich green is actually a sign of a leaf's good health, a clue to the chemicals created by photosynthesis, as a result of absorbing carbon dioxide and releasing oxygen. So unlike an artist who concentrates on light or shape in the garden, I notice the tonality, if not the beauty, of green.

About the time art classes ended, my stepfather's brother, an action painter, visited from his home in Italy. He radiated intensity, and I responded to his aura as if it were pure oxygen. When I was in my twenties, I went to an exhibition of his landscapes at an art gallery on Fifty-seventh Street in New York.

As I stood among his interpretations of the Italian countryside, all sensuality and drama and beauty, I felt as if I were encountering the elemental nature of creativity. He painted his semi-abstractions by thickly layering pigments with a palette knife onto a black background because, he explained, moving from a "black ground, towards light. That is the process of growth, of life." It is a statement of optimism but also, I now understand, the instinct of every plant. After his death, I visited an elderly artist friend of his in Salisbury, who pulled out sculptures and paintings that my uncle had given him over the years. A small oil of dark, piney Connecticut mountains against a soot-black sky and under a silvery moon evoked the fierceness of the northern winter nights I had come to know so well. And remembering the power and passion of that small painting reminded me of the importance of staying inside at my desk on a spring day.

DURING MY NINTH SPRING IN SHARON, I WAS LIVING alone and waiting for my divorce to become final. The days were sunny and cool, and there was little reason to leave town for long, so I was spending many hours in the garden. *"Very wonderful and healing,"* I wrote in my garden notebook. That April, for once, I was way ahead of nature. After sifting and spreading compost and manure on all the borders, I worked my way entirely around the yard. Afterward I enlarged the sun beds beside the barn. There were plants to divide and, of course, all the weeding and edging to do. Near the sitting area under the maple, I moved the white bleeding heart forward where it would not be overshadowed by taller ferns. As May approached, I expected to have plenty of time before the hot weather arrived for more arrangement of plants. Most of the time I was glad to be by myself. At moments, however, the backyard seemed small and the fence high. *"Overwhelming feeling of wanting to break out of my orbit, which seems so narrow right now,"* I admitted to myself, and I worried about my growing restlessness.

In the first week of May a friend telephoned to ask if I wanted to meet an eligible man, who happened to be an artist. I hesitated and then agreed. After spending a few evenings with this attractive and appealing older man, a dedicated painter and printmaker, I abandoned my gardening ambitions for the rest of the spring to be with him. In late May I jotted down in my notebook that the garden was *"quite neglected,"* but I hoped it would get along without me for a while. I weeded and deadheaded when absolutely necessary, like the July day before members of the Sharon Garden Club came to take a look. Luckily, the pale pink roses intertwined with dark purple clematis were blooming on most of the barn trellises, and I hoped that their flamboyance would divert attention from pockmarked hollyhocks and yellowed euonymus leaves. In August it was easier to give away a clump of bright pink phlox that clashed with the color of a large rosebush than figure out where to move it.

Besides neglecting my garden, I also ignored the fact that this exciting man, Robert, had never owned a garden or even gone into a garden, as far as I could tell. And, what was worse, he did not understand why anyone else would. His lack of instinct for gardening made it difficult to explain its appeal. By the end of the summer, when I began to tend the garden a little more, misunderstandings arose between us. He could not understand why I made sudden, compulsive, and conflicted, early-Sunday-morning flights from his apartment in the suburbs near New York City back to Sharon, an hour and a half away, to weed my garden.

If my urge to dig and plant was incomprehensible to him, there were habits about him that bewildered me. For years he had worked mostly from memory, indoors, with the shades drawn and the lights on, while he created canvases full of misty forests and graceful trees in shadowy fields, as he evoked a landscape's aching loveliness as well as its fragility and fleetingness. The green paint on his fingers, I noticed, came from gradually building up blackish greens, smoky greens, and grayish greens from dabs of undiluted pigments on his palette. Since windows framing the world of nature in his compositions create the impression that a darker indoors is of lesser importance than a lighter outdoors, I could not understand his preference for staying inside all day and painting imaginary landscapes, instead of enjoying real ones outside.

Realizing that the garden was increasingly taking my time and attention and keeping us apart, he tried to talk me out of it. Since I already had a garden, he asked, why did I need to keep on gardening? I thought about the question for a while, then explained that gardening, like lovemaking or painting for that matter, was an ongoing source of pleasure. During our first few months together, he repeatedly asked me when the gardening season ended, and I did not have the heart to tell him about autumn planting and winter pruning. If we were to be together, he patiently explained, he was going to lose his own gratifying hours in the studio. Next he tried another tack and asked me to regard him as a large exotic plant that needed to be fussed over. Finally, after remarking one day that he felt like a root nourished by my body, he asked if I would give up gardening. I was so torn by various emotions that I used to burst into laughter and tears at the same time because of my entangled feelings of happiness and apprehension. As I tried to explain my love of gardening, there was no question in my mind of giving it up, or, as time went on, of giving him up, either.

Gradually Robert began making etchings when he visited me in the country. One weekend he had an insight as an artist that distressed me as a writer: after agreeing to write a few paragraphs about his work for an exhibition catalog, he kept procrastinating until he decided to sketch instead; the iconography of light, line, and shadow was so enjoyable to him, he realized, he could not endure using language. But he was beginning to notice when a shrub or structure in Connecticut resembled an image in one of his prints or paintings, and then that bush or building became an object of his attention and admiration. What interested him most, I learned, were the mysterious light source and the inexplicable shadow. Some of his imaginary trees had leaves or were leafless, paired or grouped, or solitary with faint or looming shadows. Others were surrounded by explosions of leaves. They were all "dancers" and "lovers," he told me, and once, in a private moment, he admitted that "all the trees are me."

Meanwhile, I needed the garden more than ever. Working my way along the beds brought me back to myself, which, in turn, balanced the intensity and intimacy of our relationship. I was experiencing what felt like a thousand inner adjustments, so it was reassuring to see the usual seasonal progression of bloom in the everlasting cycle of nature. When weeding alone in the sweet-smelling, shadowy corners of the garden on a summer evening as the low light enhanced the colors of blooms, I felt a sense of serenity and self-possession that eluded me at other times. After falling in love, the idea of continuing to live alone seemed narrow, hollow, and absolutely unthinkable. Yet I did not want to live anywhere else but on my land in Sharon.

As we talked about getting married, nightmares about losing my house and garden dissipated during waking hours. Eventually, we agreed to be in Sharon on weekends and in his apartment overlooking the Hudson River in Westchester County on weekdays. I was so relieved about not having to choose between my home and my relationship that I did not think about other matters, like giving up glances at the garden all day or gardening on weekday afternoons. I also did not anticipate the strange sensation of traveling every few days between the colder uplands of Litchfield County to the warmer weather at the lower end of the Hudson River. Depending on which direction I drove, north to south or south to north, the season was either earlier or later, giving the impression of an extended or shortened spring or fall, but also an unnatural one. Sometimes I was wistful about leaving behind lilacs in their full glory, knowing that in an hour and a half I would only see lilacs with spent blossoms.

Yet I also felt extremely fortunate to be embarking at the age of fifty on another phase of life, a deeper, warmer, more exciting, and fuller one, as I envisioned it, with a man I loved. Still, there were difficult moments, like the evening shortly before our wedding when I sat at my desk filling out change-of-address cards and wondering what on earth I was doing. After thriving in Sharon most of the time for almost a decade, I got married again, in Manhattan, during a joyful ceremony amid the glittering lights and ribbon-bedecked greenery of a December holiday season.

ATTEMPTING TO GET ROBERT INTERESTED IN GARDENing, in the hope that we might garden together or, at least, that he would understand it better, I told him about artists who had created unique and intriguing outdoor habitats. Many of them ignored or reinvented the rules of garden design. Some have viewed gardens as gigantic still lifes, as backdrops for sculpture, or even as huge sculptures in the round. We saw several of them. In the late nineteenth century, the sculptor Augustus Saint-Gaudens planted a row of white birches as elegant verticals along a walkway at Aspet, his estate in Cornish, New Hampshire; he also used clipped evergreen hemlock hedges to form backdrops and outside galleries for his work. Saint-Gaudens interested fellow sculptor Daniel Chester French in designing the grounds at his summer estate in Stockbridge, Massachusetts. French made scale models of his ideas, observing that in both sculpture and landscape, it was important for the bones, the structure, to be correct. We also went to the landscape designer Russell Page's sculpture garden in Westchester County, where the angularity of Nevelson's black steel *Celebration II* was repeated in short, shiny spikes of dark mondo grass planted around it in the shape of a star. Yet Robert still did not grasp why an artist would want to spend time gardening.

This was difficult for me to understand because my sister has always enjoyed both studio and garden. She likes, for example, watching how time affects a painting and a planting differently. Whereas she wants a garden of hers to become "softer and wilder over time," she can stop the course of change on a canvas whenever she wishes. "I am happy to bring a painting to a static place," she says, "but I would hate that in my garden." While she welcomes "noncontrol" in the garden, many professional gardeners "create an image and work hard to keep it exactly like that" because it is what their clients demand, she points out. She wants her own gardens to be low maintenance because she lacks "the time or interest to garden more than a few days a month," while liking to watch the progression of growth. Sometimes she desires a straight line, but only when it is essential. "I love my low purple hedge which enfolds a huge swath of wild grasses—the containment of wildness—and this absolutely requires a pruned hedge, so I do it with pleasure," she says.

In a student design project for a sculpture garden of a museum in Massachusetts, she planned what she called "beautiful voids"; she used gray rocks and tall grasses as foils for future steel sculptures. "Designing for sculpture is set design, but you cannot make it so neutral that the garden experience is boring," she says. "I liked designing for an environment which encouraged the use of big swaths of things instead of fussy details." Since her plan was for a modern museum, she also felt free to choose "weird color combinations, like blackish purple foliage and masses of heavy textures like sedums," as well as specimens with twisting trunks and branches. She still prefers public plantings that exude emotion but do not "dominate the emotional state of whoever is in them," unlike formal French gardens, where she feels she has to behave herself.

One spring Robert and I went to Sissinghurst, the garden of Harold Nicolson and Vita Sackville-West, south of London. We walked on its paths around the remains of the medieval manor house, which were all odd angles and sudden views. There were gardens-within-gardens, circles and squares inside rectangles, tall poplars and flat fields, as well as clipped hedges and brick walkways restraining exuberant growth. Many of the garden's diagonals, running alongside stone ruins and an old moat, are at angles, which made our walk disorienting at first, like moving through a maze. I walked up steps in the brick tower to Vita's writing room, noting that it is high enough to see the pattern of beds below but not the weeds and wilted flowers that might have tempted her away from writing. We wandered into the enclosed white garden, which Vita had planted with soft-toned cultivars to create a "cool, almost glaucous, effect," she wrote in one of her newspaper columns. Among them was what she called "the foam of gypsophila," or baby's breath, as well as white-flowering hostas, tulips, lilies, foxgloves, columbines, dahlias, delphiniums, camellias, hydrangeas, and tree peonies in beds bordered with low hedges, all around a circular pergola that would be covered with white roses in a few weeks. A graceful gray lead sculpture of a female figure stood under the silvery green leaves of a small tree, as if giving her benediction to the lovely garden.

We sat down on a bench, and Robert was quiet for a few minutes. Then he exclaimed, "I get it. Now I get it!" Walking around the garden was like encountering an interesting mind, he remarked, an intelligence that held carefully refined ideas about space and color in horticultural terms. He told me that he at last understood what gardeners try to do—and it was like what he did in his studio. I took that moment to tell him that, without knowing it, he had been pruning all his life whenever he decided where a branch, twig, tendril, and leaf should go with a pencil, engraving tool, or paintbrush. It would be exactly the same in the garden with a pair of pruning shears, I assured him, and I was hopeful that when we got back to Connecticut, we would finally begin to garden together.

I gave him a book about pruning, but it, and the clippers he bought as a conciliatory gesture, were rarely used. My disappointment was eased when I read Gertrude Jekyll's words about a friend, a landscape painter "whose interpretation of natural beauty was of the most refined and poetical quality," she wrote with a touch of incredulousness, "but who was quite incapable of personally arranging a garden." Over time, Robert found a way to be involved with the garden by giving me large bushes for my birthdays; one September it was three magnolias and on others it was lilacs, laurels, privets, and junipers. One year his gift was a handsome old book from Barbara Farnsworth's bookstore titled *The Happiness of Our Garden*. Gradually I became glad, even grateful, that he was uninterested in decisions about the garden because, in truth, I like to make them myself.

On garden days I walk into the bright room in the barn where I keep my tools with the ease that I imagine an artist enters a studio. It is a pleasantly dirty place that is all about creativity and physicality. On a windowsill is an iron horseshoe I found in the bed by the barn and a bird's nest that fell from a tree. A paint-splattered green ladder leans against a wall near the old battered wheelbarrow my former neighbor gave me. Clay and ceramic pots are stacked here and there, as well as vine baskets from China, fruit baskets from a Manhattan greengrocer, wooden bulb crates from Holland; there are also barrels and trunks from junk shops, all holding clippers, trowels, twine, rope, stakes, sand, ashes, gloves, pebbles, fertilizers, and burlap. Shovels, saws, and rakes hang from pegs on the wall, and a long shelf and large table hold other hand tools for cutting, clipping, digging, pushing, pulling, and raking. If I were in art class again, I would paint this place a sunny yellow, a clear canary shade, because of the elation it arouses in me as I enter it before going out in the garden.

One day I visited the nearby studio of a collage artist, where I glimpsed a lot of rich red on her worktable, along with dead black and luminescent gold for a series on Hawthorne's *The Scarlet Letter.* I wanted to touch the beautiful old papers, fabrics, buttons, and other items and arrange them this way and that. Fingers tapping a keyboard are not expressive enough for me, probably because I come from a family of woodworkers and needleworkers; in fact, knitting—looping and linking a long strand of yarn around itself—is a little like writing in longhand. Once I knew a painter who put down a visual idea in watercolor in a small sketchbook every day, not unlike the way I do in my handwritten journals. One afternoon I opened my gate to the collage artist and gestured to the garden. "This is *my* color, *my* form, *my* texture!" I said to her.

At that moment I understood that gardening is my substitute for making art. And by giving me the easy enjoyment of creativity, it readies me for the writing room. While the mind may not be a sensory organ exactly like the eye, it is the link to the imagination, and in that way, gives pleasure.

nine

WOODS

―◦•◦ ◦•◦―

Feel that my whole psyche is always searching for its own balance—a certain joyousness—and felt it yesterday (a beautiful day) when I took a walk on the dirt road with the dog. Vowed to do it every day, though know I will not . . . some physical play like that seems essential for total well-being.

February 29, 1988

A FLIMSY GREEN WIRE FENCE goes all around the back of my yard, and on the long north side behind the barn it separates woods from the lawn. Running about a hundred feet, the fence makes a straight line between where I weed and where I do not, marking a dramatic demarcation point between nature acted upon and nature left alone. Over the fence everything is dense, tangled, riotous, and wild: branches of dying ash trees thrust up from where they have fallen; long runners push out from among the underbrush and put down roots wherever they land; vines wrap around trunks and grow up into the branches of ashes, maples, and black walnut trees. Little is left of the old-growth forest of tall oaks, chestnuts, elms, beeches, and the towering white pines the British used for masts of sailing ships.

This wooded lot is impenetrable except for a few weeks in late fall—after defoliation and a hard frost but before a deep snow—and in early spring before it greens up, or during a severe summer drought after leaves have shriveled. Most of the time there is no way in. If I try to get near a lovely white wildflower that I can glimpse from the grass, thorny switches and sharp twigs and sticks tear my socks and pants, knock off my hat, and pull at my hair. Unsure where to step, I try not to stumble over decaying tree limbs hidden in the tangle. The shadowy thicket is a no-man's-land where it would be easy to twist an ankle and lie helplessly in pain among the brambles and deer ticks, with nothing to do but imagine what the forest once was and what my yard would be again, if it was left alone for fifty or a hundred years.

It is surprising, I suppose, to find a fragment of forest in the middle of a village, hemmed in on all sides by swing sets, woodpiles, compost bins, garbage cans, old sheds, and abandoned cars. It is not a large area—less than an acre—but it has always been regarded as out-of-bounds except by small boys, at least in the memories of older people in town. A number of years ago I noticed a boy, most likely a neighbor's son, exploring the woods, probably playing Daniel Boone or an Indian brave. Years earlier another neighbor, Sally Jenkins, had found the woods too overgrown to venture into when she was a little girl. Instead of taking a shortcut through the undergrowth from her home on New Street to her parents' grocery store on Main Street, she went along a footpath through what became my yard. The neighbors next door to me owned the acre of trees until they sold it off to sisters who built a small house on the opposite end of it in the 1970s. The latest owner is an absentee landlord, who might like to sell off the thicket apart from the house, but zoning regulations do not permit such small parcels in the village anymore.

I had put up the lightweight fencing around the back of the yard to keep my dog in and wild animals out. Once a gray rabbit squeezed under the wire; the cocker spaniel chased it, until the frightened creature lay panting with exhaustion against the fence, unable to find a way out, while the dog gently sniffed it and wagged her tail. When I went outside and discovered the imbroglio, I put on leather work gloves to guard against bites and carried the rabbit back to its briar patch. Since I never again saw a rabbit in the backyard, I assume that cats and fiercer village dogs than mine finished it off, along with most of the field mice, chipmunks, woodchucks, and raccoons. Despite these animals' absence in the little woodland, I am always aware of its intense aliveness because of all the squirrels, crows, and the other birds that dart in and out of the leafy canopy.

In winter when the woods are virtually leafless, I imagine

how they would look without any weedy growth. I visualize a glen full of ferns, hostas, primroses, jack-in-the-pulpits, and wildflowers like the white-blossomed trillium, which is colloquially called birthroot or bloodroot, and other shade-tolerant plants. In my imagination, golden viridescent light would filter through leaves to the forest floor, illuminating a cluster of large-leafed plants here and a few tiny flowers there. Sweet woodruff and speckled pulmonaria would be among them, since they have already started to move from my garden through the fence and into the woods; the fence, in fact, is no impediment at all. In my mind's eye, the struggling stand of trees would resemble a scene in a nineteenth-century landscape of an idealized American wilderness that was painted when the original, old forest was rapidly disappearing. I would also be able to walk through my fantasy woodland garden any time of year and sit and look around on a secluded bench.

Instead of this imaginary garden, I have an ongoing struggle with the woods. Growth persistently pushes itself out of the shadows, through the porous wire barricade, and into the sunlight on my side of the fence. In early spring I hack my way along the other side of the fence in an effort to keep the determined green wall within bounds. I want to stop its advance before it ruins where I work so hard to clip, cut, weed, edge, and prune in my attempt to arrange nature. Since at times I even fear its unrelenting force, I like to fling the sticks and branches it drops onto my lawn back at it. After the foliage leafs out in spring and thickens in summer, I work my way along my mowed side of the fence with clippers and hand saws to attack the tenacious tendrils and offshoots that press against and poke through the openings in the fence. Sometimes I push a gloved hand through a wire square to try to pull up a poison ivy vine or a weed with a seedpod about to open. As I move down the divide between grass and woodland, the thin fence reminds me of the porous barrier between mental awareness and oblivion, the potent place where new ideas germinate.

When I wonder how much naturalness there should be in nature, I remember the doctors' office on Main Street with its neglected garden. Someone is hired to rake it once in a while, but not nearly often enough. It is enclosed by a broken white picket fence and has peonies, phlox, and lilies that no one bothers to weed around, deadhead, fertilize, water, or prune. Even so, the peonies manage to produce a few blossoms every June; sometimes an opulent red bloom rests between fractured pickets as if on a guillotine. Phlox that have reverted to garish magenta compete with orange tiger lilies for light. Scraggly weed trees—mostly black walnuts—reach higher into the branches of other trees every year. A red Japanese maple has many dead branches; limbs from a pear tree lie where they have dropped. Every year the goldenrod, poison ivy, Queen Anne's lace, and dandelions make more headway in a kind of awful experiment in undergardening. Watching this weed garden makes me understand that after ground has been gardened and abandoned, it takes time for nature to recover its grace. When I weed on my hands and knees in my yard to keep it from reverting to weeds and woods, I remember that I am always negotiating the line between too little or too much control in the garden as well as outside it.

After getting a severe rash on my arms, I decided to get rid of the poison ivy along the fence once and for all. When I walked toward shelves of pesticides and herbicides at a garden center, however, the strong chemical stench overwhelmed me. Reaching for a deadly chemical that plants draw into their roots, I remembered Nathaniel Hawthorne's Gothic tale "Rappaccini's Daughter," which describes a botanic garden in Padua, Italy, full of magnificent but malignant plants artificially propagated by a deranged scientist named Rappaccini. His beautiful young daughter, Beatrice, had fallen victim to his frightening experiments: she alone could safely get near the poisonous plants, but because her breath and touch were lethal to others, she was alone and very lonely. The spray can of herbicide in my hand seemed to be, as Hawthorne had written in his prescient work of science fiction at a time when plants were first being hybridized, one of the "new varieties of poison, more horribly deleterious than Nature."

My garden has its share of borers, slugs, scales, and ticks, and I would not mind if my breath, like Beatrice's, caused them to drop dead instantly. But poisons sprayed on leaves or sprinkled on soil also kill or keep away bugs and other beings beneficial to the biosphere, like earthworms, bees, ladybugs, spiders, snakes, and toads. Since toads eat slugs, I try to lure them into the garden by placing an upside-down pot to shelter them among the greenery where water collects in a stone. Sometimes attracting these creatures to the garden is also a matter of aesthetics, like wanting the pleasure of watching butterflies flit around a blooming bush as if they were wind-borne blossoms.

I was not sure what was worse: dangerous poisons or devouring pests. I had to do something about stubborn scale on the evergreen euonymus vines that camouflaged the cement foundation of the house. Clusters of scale, a minuscule insect that secretes a hard shell, were turning branches whitish and yellowing glossy green leaves. Another kind of scale had attacked the magnolias so severely that branches turned brown and had to be amputated. Robert, to my surprise, removed a lot of the scale by hand, but I still had to take preventive measures. Even though spraying made me uneasy, I would reluctantly put on a long-sleeved shirt, long pants, goggles, rubber gloves, and a nose-and-mouth mask, then filled a spray tank with horticultural oil, sometimes laced with a toxin, to suffocate the insects.

At such times I felt like Hawthorne's Rappaccini, a sickly individual who was so afraid of the poisons in his own garden that he put on a mask and gloves before venturing out into it. "It was strangely frightful," Hawthorne had written, "to see this air of insecurity in a person cultivating a garden, that most simple and innocent of human toils." As if predicting the widespread fumes that would pollute the air a century later, he then asked: "Was this Eden, then, the Eden of the present world?" Perhaps the price of pristine greenery is too high for our endangered environment, but I was not ready to give up all pesticides and insecticides just yet.

THE BIT OF WOODS NEXT TO MY BACKYARD IS SO SMALL and surrounded by so much village life that it seems more like a habitat in a zoo than a frightening place to be. But what if the entire continent of North America were as wild? Only a few of the earliest settlers valued the wilderness, like a young French-woman traveling through Massachusetts in 1794, who wrote in her memoirs of her admiration for the wildflowers. Nineteen-year-old Madame de la Tour du Pin had been a lady-in-waiting to Queen Marie-Antoinette before fleeing the French Revolution. "The road through these magnificent forests was only wide enough for two carriages," she remembered. "In the more open areas, there were thickets of flowering rhododen-drons, some of them purple, others pale lilac, and roses of every kind. The flowers made a vivid splash of color against the grassland, which was itself studded with mosses and flowering plants, while in the low-lying parts . . . every kind of water plant was in full flower. This unspoiled nature enchanted me to such an extent that I spent the entire day in ecstasy."

Most colonists, however, feared the forest, for good rea-son: screeching branches in the wind, rustlings in the under-brush, and moving shadows in the moonlight might have meant the approach of wild animals or hostile Indians. To make matters worse, Puritans like the Reverend Cotton Mather preached that the shadowy wilderness was a godforsaken place where dragons, devils, flying serpents, and other supernatural demons might tempt people into pagan ways, especially in faraway settlements like Sharon.

A generation later, railroads began moving through forests, including to Sharon Station, near the village, and much of the landscape of New England rapidly turned into fields, pastures, meadows, and gardens. As the old-growth forest disappeared, a number of American artists and writers developed a newfound appreciation for it. Nathaniel Hawthorne, who wrote *The Scarlet Letter* in what was then the wilds of western Massachusetts, described in the novel a forbidding "great black forest" that had encircled a small settlement a generation earlier. But in Hawthorne's narrative the wilderness was also an embracing "mother-forest," a sheltering place of privacy and beauty. It was where his heroine, Hester Prynne, found refuge from the disapproving eyes of the town, and where her young out-of-wedlock daughter gathered berries and wildflowers—violets, wood anemones, and scarlet columbines—and befriended birds, squirrels, foxes, and wolves.

Hawthorne's friend Ralph Waldo Emerson wrote essays and sermons about feeling inexplicably uplifted, hopeful, and happy when walking through the familiar woods near Concord in eastern Massachusetts. His emotions were aroused as intensely as his thoughts by the world of nature, he claimed, while his egotism vanished and his spirituality strengthened, resulting in an exhilarating sense of wholeness. "In the presence of nature a wild delight runs through the man, in spite of real sorrows," he wrote in his influential manifesto *Nature.* "In the woods, we return to reason and faith. There I feel that nothing can befall me in life,—no disgrace, no calamity (leaving me my eyes), which nature cannot repair." After Emerson invited the young Henry David Thoreau to build a cabin on his land near Walden Pond, Thoreau went even further in celebrating the nearby woods, even though he bemoaned the loss of its wildlife. The rumble of the passing Boston train sounded like a death knell to him.

Although Thoreau famously wrote that "in Wildness is the preservation of the World," he was actually more comfortable in the woods and wetlands he knew than in the wilds of northern New England. While climbing Maine's Mount Katahdin, he discovered a shockingly desolate "inhuman Nature," more like a stern stepmother than a smiling "Mother Earth," as he put it. "Perhaps I most fully realized that this was primeval, untamed, and forever untamable *Nature,*" he explained. "This was the Earth of which we have heard, made out of Chaos and Old Night." Thoreau, who could also hear band music and celebratory gunshot in Concord from his cabin on the Fourth of July, was, like many others before and after him, actually most at ease in what is called the middle landscape.

It is an old preference, and one I probably share as well, judging from my fantasy about transforming the woods alongside my backyard into a woodland garden. In backgrounds of medieval altarpieces portraying Madonnas and saints, prettified landscapes outside walled towns are pleasingly planted, and even the woods look agreeably benign. Roderick Nash, professor emeritus of history and environmental studies at the University of California, offers a theory in *Wilderness and the American Mind* about mankind being hardwired to feel safer, and thereby happier, on hills with wide views, where human eyes and brains have more of an evolutionary advantage than in dark forests.

If people instinctively respond positively, even passionately, to the openness of the in-between place—neither garden nor forest but an appealing balance of both—perhaps this is why when the view on the road between Sharon and Salisbury was threatened, there was an outcry from residents of both towns. In the middle distance from the overlook, there is a sloping meadow with two trees on it and, just beyond, a lake lying below rolling pastures and woods and, farther away, ridge after ridge of undulating hills. From the rise on the road, the faraway trees look as if they might be fruit trees, but they are actually gigantic old oaks rooted in a forty-acre field. In winter the twin trees, which stand in exquisite relationship to each other, throw black shadows on the snow, while in summer they are balls of greenness that turn to russet in the fall. This gentle vision of arcadia, of arching sky, sheltering hills, and shining water, strikes a strong emotional chord in passersby.

After the field was sold to a realtor who planned to build on it, townspeople raised hundreds of thousands of dollars so the Sharon Land Trust could buy the acreage. Half the money came from a ninety-nine-year-old philanthropist who had first seen the view when he attended nearby Hotchkiss School as a boy. One sunny summer day a few months after the fund drive ended, a huge celebratory picnic was held at a farm overlooking the twin oaks field. The old man wore a dapper straw hat and fingered a silver-tipped cane, while a six-foot-long cake with frosting replicating the scenery was sliced up, and bands played and speakers made congratulatory toasts to the rescue of the field and to one another.

It was a wonderful party, but was it a real victory?

That day I heard no mention of the huge, high-voltage electrical towers that march down the hill and into the view. Nor did I see much reference to the steel behemoths in paintings and photographs of this scene made by more than a hundred artists as part of the fund-raising effort. Now little green-and-white farmland preserve plaques are nailed to fence posts at the bottom of the field. One autumn afternoon I walked past them and all the way to the top. From there I looked through a hedgerow and saw a large house and lawn on the other side; from my vantage point, I could also see many other homes as well as power lines and roads all around the field. For the first time in more than a century, the regrown woodlands of central New England are contracting again, making way for new houses and the cultivated land around them. Looking up at the highway above the field, I could see the steady stream of traffic that passes through Sharon every day, including enormous trucks that downshift deafeningly as they approach the stop sign near my house, the sign that was meant to divert them to other routes. The town of Sharon has been threatened but has so far avoided being sliced by a natural-gas pipeline and selected the site of a radioactive waste dump, but I still dread so-called progress as much as my ancestors feared the forest.

EVEN THOUGH I LOVE LOOKING AT THE MIDDLE DISTANCE from the overlook, I also want to be in the woods, where, like the land alongside my garden, nature is left alone. When I feel like rebelling against the demands of my domesticated sliver of land, or as they lessen in fall and winter, it is a relief to set out by foot on a mountain trail or a country road. In fact, starting out on a walk often makes me feel like Houdini released from a box. The dirt road I like best was probably an old Indian footpath, judging from the way it meanders alongside a stream. Right after the pavement ends, it crosses a fast-flowing salmon stream, Mill Brook, whose name reveals its past. Walking away from the village, the way is mostly uphill. On one side is a steep forested hillside, and on the other is a sloping field beyond a dark, leafy veil, punctuated by dark spikes of tree trunks and telephone poles. Along the road are tumbled mossy rocks from old stone walls. I liked to let my dog off the leash, and let her run and lap from a mountain stream before darting excitedly from one side of the road to the other. The few feet of packed dirt keep the dense green walls of growth at bay much better than my flimsy wire fence at home.

In winter, snow sits like mounds of white frosting on dark pine boughs, while stands of white birches lighten the darkness of the woods. One day during a February thaw, the woods were almost all brown and expectantly hushed, as if saving their strength for spring. In a few weeks pale dabs of swelling buds on branches would turn the woodland into a pointillist painting. Every year skunk cabbage leaves and yellow trout lilies rise from rivulets of snowmelt beside the rutted road. By summer buttercups, feverfew, blue cornflowers, and airy Queen Anne's lace open in patches of sunlight alongside the road, the same spots where wild purple asters will take their place in autumn. It's odd that what I admire as wildflowers along the road I regard as weeds in the garden. My mother, who allowed a wildflower field to grow in front of her house, rarely condemned anything as a weed. "A weed is only a plant out of place," she liked to say, quoting an old aphorism. Some plants are almost always weeds, like poison ivy and invasive plants, like the alarmingly aggressive giant hogweed, which has recently appeared in northwestern Connecticut.

Undoubtedly, the woods alongside the road look more beautiful and less menacing than those behind my barn because they are not the enemy of the garden. Red and yellow leaves in the fall make me see, as if with new eyes, the gracefulness of rounded foliated crowns. One October afternoon I was stopped by the sight of a great blue heron standing motionless in fallen yellow leaves beside a glittering brook, one of many herons that inhabit the woods in summer. Flocks of wild turkeys often fly up in explosions of black feathers while my dog, nose in the air, quivers all over. Or, as I round a bend, white-tailed deer might leap across the road. Coyotes and bobcats have followed the deer back to the region, and reports of mountain lion sightings are frequent. Although I worry when I hear gunshots during hunting season, I am usually wearing a flaming-orange hunter's vest, so I continue on. While the sound of guns is worrisome, so is the possibility of encountering a lion or a black bear. Thoreau liked getting temporarily lost in his tamed woods near Concord, but I stay on the road because of the frisson of fear I feel in this regrown forest.

Despite my apprehension, the rhythm of my footsteps lulls me and I lose myself in daydreaming. As the road winds uphill—curving, straightening, rising—it is like the pathway of a thought. One day it occurred to me to use old-fashioned methods to get rid of bugs, like strong tea or icy or soapy water. I later learned from old garden books and organic-gardening manuals that garlic, chives, and mint repel aphids, while the odor of geraniums repulses Japanese beetles, and the smell of rosemary wards off slugs. It is all right, I thought, for a person to possess a landscape as long as it is done without strong poisons; I decided to use oils and fungicides when absolutely necessary, but to avoid pesticides. Instead, I would do the disgusting work of pulling fleshy pink borers from iris tubers with my bare fingers, flicking clumps of copulating Japanese beetles into cans of water, and enticing slugs to drown in shallow containers of beer.

As I walked on the dirt road another afternoon, I remembered that the human race has always pontificated about nature, interpreting it as benign or malevolent at one time or another. When wilderness covered most of the earth, Aristotle philosophized that the natural world existed for the sake of mankind, a viewpoint that remained largely unchallenged until recently. An old bird feeder that was once in a grandmother's garden is now in my cutting garden; it has a ceramic depiction of Saint Francis in a monk's brown robe with his arms magnanimously outstretched toward a flock of white birds flying against a blue background. It reminds me that while the Old Testament decrees that descendants of Adam and Eve should have "dominion over the fish of the sea, and over the fowl of the air, and over every living thing that moveth upon the earth," in the New Testament Saint Francis says that birds and beasts have spirits, and I agree with him.

After about two miles the road crosses another bridge over another brook, where I am usually ready to turn around and go downhill toward my car. One day I recalled that Supreme Court Justice William O. Douglas had created a wilderness bill of rights, believing that wild nature, or deep nature, is part of the American birthright. For more than two centuries, the western frontier had represented the right to be alone as well as the chance to begin all over again, the impulses that had made me move to the country. When I get back to Main Street, I usually feel better about whatever was bothering me before, and I know I am in trouble when dark thoughts do not dissipate during a long walk.

A few years ago, a young couple from Manhattan bought a house right off the dirt road. Soon afterward they petitioned town selectmen to declare it officially "scenic" under a new town ordinance. Not long ago it was little more than a rough track through the woods, and it is still perilously narrow for passing cars and trucks. To realtors, road crews, firemen, ambulance drivers, and a few residents of the road, this is a problem. There have been a few fatal accidents. Nonetheless, the Malleys managed to get virtually all the landowners along the road to sign the petition, undoubtedly including the runners, men on mountain bikes, and women with dogs and on horseback whom I pass on the road. A dissenter at a town hall meeting was outvoted, and the petition was passed. Now the road can no longer be widened, flattened, or straightened except for reasons of safety. "The safety clause is a time bomb," worries Steve Malley, who, along with his wife and young son, drives two hours to their retreat in the woods almost every weekend.

This weekender is glad that the twists and turns of the dirt road slow down cars and trucks but, even so, when I hear a motor, I move way to the side. One time my dog was running down a driveway into the path of an oncoming car, and I ran out into the road with arms outstretched until I had leashed her. Wheels leave behind dust and exhaust, flattened snakes, dead squirrels, and maimed chipmunks, as well as beer bottles, cigarette cartons, and fast-food wrappers. I usually bring along a bag for the litter, since the detritus of the town seems intolerable in the woods. Yet if this road and the twin oaks field had no legal protection at all, the dirt would eventually be paved and the hillside partitioned into building lots. While nature sometimes needs the proverbial town with its rules and regulations, townspeople always need the presence of nature. The exchange is not equal, and nature gives far more to us than we give to it.

Working away in the garden, I wonder whether a gardener can improve on nature at all. Or whether the garden and grove give meaning to each other. The thicket over my fence may look like a kind of green chaos, but it obeys the underlying order of natural law. The woods are as wonderful to me, in truth, as the most masterful garden. Anyone with a bird's-eye view of the backyards in town might get the impression that they are the work of a deranged Mother Nature. When my garden is full of white and pastel bulbs in early spring, for instance, my neighbors have masses of bright red and yellow varieties. Sometimes it gives me mental vertigo to question the validity of gardening while, at the same time, continuing to adore it.

Near and middle distances each have their importance, but the ultimate view is seeing the earth from above. When I flew across the country one winter, the rivers of North America made intricate gray curlicues that were more graceful than the straight lines of superhighways linking clusters of dwellings to cities. From the air I could see vast agricultural circles below that were mechanically irrigated, fertilized, and doused with chemicals, making pretty patterns in the snow. Floating over the land were drifts of brown haze under a layer of white wispy clouds, but where the airplane was moving, the atmosphere was a pure celestial blue. Photographs taken by orbiting satellites farther away from the earth show what looks like a deceptively peaceable round planet—pale pink, light blue, and soft green—and as fragile as a flower. We can continue to destroy our earth, I reflected, or we can try to save the small speck that is always turning and circling in the brightness and the blackness.

t e n

OUTSIDE

⸺•◄ ►•⸺

This regimen of working in
the garden in the early a.m. is
thrilling—to begin and end
the daylight hours like that!
I'm also doing more good
gardening, because I have
more energy in the early a.m.
It also seems like stolen time,
private and pure time,
certainly a gift to myself.

May 12, 1993

IT WAS AT DAWN ON A WINTER
morning when I first glimpsed a
deer in the back of the yard. Initially, I was thrilled at the sight of
such a lovely wild creature so close
to the house, but when I came to my
senses and saw that it was grazing
on my evergreens, I ran outside
in my bathrobe, waving my arms
and clapping my hands like a madwoman. The tawny animal stood
as still as a statue, stared at me for
a long moment, then sauntered
toward the fence alongside the
woods and effortlessly leaped over it
while flipping its white tail at me.

I had assumed that a garden in the middle of the village was safe from large wildlife, so the sight of the deer astonished me. Perhaps I had been naive: its predators, like wolves and hunters, have lessened in number, and I knew that the native white-tailed deer had returned in droves to browse the border-line areas between woods and clearings, especially to eat pampered ornamentals in outlying areas of the township. Some gardeners outside the village had put up ten-foot-high netting or electrified fences around their properties, while others had given up gardening altogether. Until that morning, however, I had not seen the animals near Main Street. Now I worried that they would eventually eat everything I had planted, and I would be back where I had started, with little more than an empty expanse of grass.

The deer I saw that day, or perhaps it was another in its herd, returned the following winters, usually at dawn or dusk or in the moonlight, to nibble prickly leaves of hollies and rhododendron greenery curled up in the cold. At first they appeared in the yard only during winter when leafless woods offer little to eat, leaving behind piles of little round pellets and dainty cleft hoofprints crisscrossing the snow. Before long deer began to appear in daylight, too. One sunny winter afternoon, I glanced out a back window and glimpsed the hindquarters of a huge mammal gnawing on the evergreen euonymus vines clinging to the foundation of the house. When I tapped on the glass, it lifted its delicate head and blinked a glittering black eye; after becoming motionless for a startled second, it clattered its hooves on the wooden boards of the sitting area and loped toward the trees.

When I heard that a lone deer can devour a ton and a half of vegetation a year, I realized it would be foolhardy to plant more evergreens. In an attempt to discourage the animals from munching on what was already planted, I tried repellent sprays and hung wind chimes on trees; I also threw dog droppings into the woods and tied up human hair in old stockings and hung it from overhanging branches. The denuded hollies had died, but I hopefully wrapped the laurels and rhododendrons in bird netting. The deer, however, managed to tear off and chew—if not swallow—leaves through the plastic mesh, so the almost leafless laurels, their favorites, were soon surrounded by piles of masticated bits of green. Nevertheless, there was something about the hungry herbivores that moved me, a feeling that was reinforced when I learned that they survive for only a few years in the wild. Even so, I dreaded what would happen if they started to forage on the flowers during the growing season.

A couple of months later, a neighbor glimpsed a large herd of deer on the green while walking her dog early in the morning. A few had apparently wandered down my driveway, beheading the big hybrid purple crocuses that I had laboriously planted in the fall. Devastated, I remembered a gray March afternoon after moving to Sharon, when the sky was dull, the ground was covered with blackened snow, and the sidewalk was gritty from sandy slush sprayed by passing traffic. *"Everything is ugly,"* I wrote that day. *"Dirty snow, brown grass—yet today, a warm day, I detect a slight greening of the grass."* As I walked home, I noticed with disgust the grime that had splattered and streaked the front windows and clapboards of my house. Then I suddenly stopped, causing my dog's leash to jerk and her head to twist around. On the sodden brown grass were wisps of lavender and yellow—the slender petals of small species crocuses planted by an earlier owner. My mentality was still a winter one, and I was prepared for more cold and more grayness, so the appearance of the fragile blossoms was a miraculous sight. Spotting those brave little signs of spring, especially during a February thaw, always startled me out of my winter stoicism, so I did not want deer to destroy them.

After my spaniel died at the age of sixteen and I buried her in the yard, the deer became bolder. Early one summer morning I saw a great tan animal lying down in the back of the yard, resting on the grass as if my garden was its own habitat, which, I suppose, it was. When I went outside, the deer twitched its large ears, stared at me, then slowly stood up and walked toward the woods. Over the next few months this deer and others returned to behead the daylilies at the far end of the yard and then to browse nearer to the barn. I suppose it was inevitable that the beasts (as the word *deer* means in Old English) would eventually do what I had long feared: move close to the house when the garden was at its peak to nip off the big buds of the tall white trumpet lilies and other treasured flowers, just as they were about to open.

Yet I was still ambivalent about the otherworldly wildlife that appeared in the backyard. Their appeal was intensified when I saw a few paragraphs in the weekly newspaper about the sighting of "a pure white deer" that had emerged from the woods to drink from the river "like something in a fairy tale or a dream," the observer wrote. The incident reminded me of the unicorn tapestries in the Cloisters, a museum of medieval art in upper Manhattan that is part of the Metropolitan Museum of Art. Woven in Belgium around 1500, the seven tapestries tell a sad tale about the capture of a white unicorn, a legendary creature with a single horn in the center of its forehead. It was hunted because it was believed that an essence in its horn protected against poison and disease. In the old story of mankind's conquest of the wild, the gigantic tapestries vividly portray a larger-than-life stag that looks like an albino deer struggling for life, and finally as a tamed animal sitting chained to a tree and enclosed by a fence. These ancient fabrics also have beautifully rendered spring flowers and fruit trees, all miraculously bearing and blooming at the same time. These flowers that existed before hybrids—pansies, violets, irises, roses, lilies, and many more—all grow in my garden today and remind me again that some aspects of nature are everlasting.

THE ATTEMPT OF GARDENERS TO WREST BEAUTY FROM nature is about arrangement as much as anything else: planting flowers together whose shapes and colors enhance one another. Perfect placement creates a third effect by sending a pulse of pleasure to the brain. It happens when low-growing lungworts create a layer of soft blue blossoms under bright pink daffodils; when dark purple clematises open on a trellis with pale pink roses; when yellow candelabra primroses flatter tiny blue florets of the Jacob's ladder; when frothy masses of forget-me-nots set off stiff iris spears above them; and when dark blue floral cups of the great irises emerge from lower clusters of barely pink peonies. One summer I exulted in the garden notebook: *"East sun bed is gorgeous with pink roses and blue spiky flowers in bloom at the same time."* Besides a plan on paper and the polite behavior of plants, it takes exact amounts of rain, light, and heat for buds to open together and result in a few days of rare beauty. It might also, I was startled to realize, take more hours of gardening to create an ideal combination than the number of hours it lasted, but that was of little importance to me. After all, by then I had become a gardener.

When I lacked time to move plants around the yard in search of better combinations, it meant putting up with another season of disappointments—clashing colors, smaller clumps behind larger ones, and the skimpiness of under-planted places. In the opposite of the enhancement effect, some plants diminish the appearances of others or are diminished themselves, like when an ivory rose looked anemic near a pure white phlox, and when a candy pink rosebush clashed with a blush pink climber above it. *"Pinks of little rose and hardy geranium clash,"* I wrote in my garden notes. *"Which should go? If either? Or plant something between them?"* Another time I admitted: *"I've lost plenty of plants, but I've also thrown out those I dislike, like stiff lupine, for those I like better and which act better or are more beautiful and better behaved."* The rule of the eye is harsh, and as I tossed out thriving plants that were in the wrong places, aesthetically speaking, I tried to remember the words of Vita Sackville-West about the necessity of being ruthless in the garden.

Vita, an aristocrat, believed in a botanical hierarchy, ranging from common to worthy types of plants. Once selected for her garden, a specimen had to perform to her standards by flourishing, enlarging, and blooming abundantly on schedule. If not, a perennial only plodding along would be uprooted or a tree casting too much shade would be cut down. "I feel that one of the secrets of good gardening is always to remove, ruthlessly, any plant one doesn't like," she wrote in one of her newspaper columns, and to replace it with something better. "That is the only way to garden. The true gardener must be brutal, and imaginative for the future." Unsurprisingly, it appeared as if "every plant in the garden was delighted to be there," observed one of its many visitors, Sir John Gielgud, according to Jane Brown in *Vita's Other World.*

On the other hand, I was realizing that a too strictly imposed plan overlooks the valid willfulness of plants. I had to remember that I was only the referee, the human being who weeded and pinched back and watched everything grow. If I was patient and paid close attention, perennials would let me know where they wanted to be. I vowed to become more vigilant about where I planted them—as well as where I put myself. After visiting Sharon only on weekends the year after Robert and I were married, we worked out a way to spend more time in the country so I could do more gardening. Now that I have more humility and horticultural knowledge, I am better at sensing which plants to restrain and which to let run, like the appealing wild ginger ground cover that is moving into all the shadowy places.

After a while I gave up my attempt at absolute dominance of the garden for a number of reasons. One of them was the presence of the voracious deer—like the weather, they are a wild card: able to destroy in a matter of minutes what has taken years to grow. Instead of a rigid plan, I began to adhere to design principles, like trying to contrast curvaceous forms of flowers with straight edges of borders in a satisfying interplay of restraint and abandon, control and freedom. The existence of opposites, which we hold within ourselves, is expressed by edging a flower bed. (In fact, òne evening a speaker at the Sharon Garden Club remarked that defining the boundary between flowers and grass is the best and fastest way to make a garden look good.)

I also abandoned meticulous planning because recording everything was taking too long. More important, trying to pin down living plants on paper inhibited moments of intuition and impulse, when I suddenly knew what to do. If I watched and waited, inspiration usually arrived as an entire idea, as if it were inevitable. This happened one morning when I suddenly understood how to solve the problems of encroaching pachysandra, struggling grass, and sump pump drainage under the maple: rock pits and pathways alongside rows of hostas (underplanted with wild ginger) on either side of a wood-chip path. In a matter of hours I had ordered a dozen sweet-smelling white hostas and a truckload of topsoil, and all I had to do was find enough rocks for the paths and for retaining walls at the end of the raised hosta beds.

I remembered seeing a ROCKS FOR SALE sign on a nearby road. A steep hillside is strewn with gigantic granite rocks, some lying sideways and others balanced precariously on their edges, like an amphitheater where some barbaric performance is about to begin. Underbrush is partially hacked away and tree trunks are scattered about. Flat slabs form huge steps, rounded ones make rock walls and pillars, and even an archway, while pinkish stone lions stand guard like sentinels. While the spectacle is totemic, it is also alarming because it seems as if at any moment gravity will send one or another of the boulders crashing down onto the road. After I called the telephone number on the sign and spoke with the owner, Michael Rost, he built my retaining walls within days. He referred to his stone-strewn hillside as a rock garden, but I thought he was wrong: gardens are not dangerous—they are safe places between wild nature and the walls of a house.

After giving up my detailed garden plan, I was better able to put gardening in its place. I try to keep up with the seasons

so I am not overwhelmed, like spraying dormant oil on the euonymus before it leafs out, uprooting weeds before they release
seeds, and shading the shallow roots of rhododendrons with
pine branches before the heat of summer arrives. I like to sit in
the shade of the maple with Robert or a friend or a book on
steamy summer afternoons and now and then glance at the
garden. At such times I understand that the enjoyment of
looking is nothing compared with the pleasure of gardening—
and that I would much rather garden than have a Garden.
When I have time or money, I do more, and at other times I
just keep the garden going. It is a choice of process over perfection, not that the latter is ever possible.

Regardless of how the garden grows, it is a place to tap
into the vitality of nature. What is ordinary, yet also extraordinary, about spring in New England is the way it arrives so
abruptly after winter. The sighting of the tiny crocuses in front
of the house is a reminder to look along the fence in back,
where the weak, wintry sunlight lingers the longest. There I
inevitably find the snow gone, and the large white crocuses
with golden stamens blooming away under dry brown leaves.
It is impossible for me to ignore buried blooms, so I get a basket from the barn, pull on a pair of gloves, and gingerly begin
to uncover them. At such times it is easy to forget that a late-
winter snowstorm may very well entomb the blossoms and
brown their pristine petals. Whenever that happens, I feel as
though icy flakes are falling on my bare skin, and I blame myself for being too eager to remove the protective leaves. Mean-

while, I stay indoors in an unsettled state, waiting for snow to melt and spring to start once again.

IT ALSO BECAME EVIDENT THAT CREATING GARDEN ROOMS was the best way to structure my long, narrow half acre. Right behind the house was the place to begin. It was already bordered on three sides by fencing and buildings, and only needed a fourth wall, a wall of greenery, which would also be a backdrop for flowers. This wall would go across the yard near the end of the barn, where the backyard would not look unnaturally broken in two, and have a wide opening to walk through. Retaining walls were built, then I shoveled compost into the new beds and planted rows of evergreen boxwood bushes. The boxwood's little leaves are distasteful to deer, so I was optimistic about my wall not being eaten. As the bushes grew into hedges, a sense of enclosure was enhanced by the large lilacs and magnolias rising behind them.

For a while I resisted closing the opening in the green wall, but it was an entranceway for deer moving into the garden room. Deer repellents were not working, and the Humane Society of the United States affirmed what Thomas Jefferson had known more than two centuries ago—that the only way to keep deer out of a garden is with walls and fences with gates; he had used them to keep the native deer out of his gardens at Monticello, at a time when there were far fewer inhabitants but as many deer in the East as today. Knowing what I had to do, I began moving prized perennials from the cutting garden to the flower beds within the garden room. At first I attached wire fencing to garden stakes across the opening, and then I ordered a gate, with an arbor for the gap in the boxwood barrier. Since I was of two minds about the deer, it was a triage approach: an attempt to safeguard the garden near the house and a willingness to sacrifice the plantings in the back of the yard. Once when heavy snow weighed down branches of the boxwoods, I spotted deer tracks on the near side of the gate, but there was little there to damage, and I believed that the garden was safer than before.

Since the tall fence I had put in years earlier was rotting and rickety, I replaced it with another board-on-board fence that provides ventilation for vegetation. Along with the new gateway, it was stained the same inky green as the house's shutters and doors. A darker green than any vegetation I had ever seen, I had hoped it would look all right. I was apprehensive the October day the fence went up, aware that its darkness would frame the plants and flowers in an entirely different way. Afterward, I was relieved to see that the color set off the purple asters and white windflowers blooming beside it. I also saw that the arch over the gate framed this view or that from the windows of the house, and I started to look for a bench or birdbath to attract the eye. In winter the straight lines of the dark fence in the snow act as a transition between the house and the garden. And the four walls of the garden room do not make me feel fenced in at all: there is endless sky overhead and thousands of miles of earth underneath.

By autumn it always seems as if the iris week, the peony week, the rose week, the lily week, and all the other summer weeks have passed quickly. As the last of the fall flowers open, including mauve chrysanthemums with yellow centers from my mother's garden, the soil stays warm while the air cools off, so it is an ideal time for working outside. It is also borrowed time: a warm afternoon of planting bulbs may be followed by a morning of shoveling snow. *"Snow! And I have not raked leaves in back of yard, cut grass in back, raked leaves in front, shredded leaves, put compost on beds, cut down dead perennials because last two weekends had locked gray skies and I was uninspired,"* I wrote in my notebook one November. Almost every day that time of year more leaves and stalks are blackened by nighttime frosts. I try to find the time to spread compost and manure over the brown beds, as if to tuck them in for winter. It is all so hurried, because every afternoon there is less and less light.

Usually the garden is a place of stillness. There is only the faint sense of blood moving through the brain, and the vibration of air before it becomes wind. Some sounds are welcome, like the raucousness of geese as they fly low over the house. Others are unwelcome, like the scream of the siren on the roof of the nearby fire station. Yet I am grateful when the little helicopter from Hartford Hospital roars in over the treetops like a gigantic bird toward the small hospital around the corner; I am grateful it is coming, and that it is not coming for me. As it rises and races out of earshot, silence returns to the garden again except for the hourly tolling of church bells. The number of rings is always surprising since they signal how rapidly time passes in the garden. On late fall afternoons four tolls send me back inside.

The light lures me outside on bright winter days, and, once there, I remember that the season is not the end of gardening. It is enjoyable to gather twigs for kindling, clip brittle clematis, and cut off misshapen, leafless branches. Back inside I sometimes ask myself what, really, is a garden? To the naturalist a plot of ground is an interdependent web of flora and fauna. A poet is likely to find that a flowery bower is a place of inspiration rich with symbolism. Cultivated landscapes make the philosopher speculate about the relationship of humanity to nature. A secluded garden suggests to a lover a private place for a romantic tryst. To an artist a garden is an interplay of color and form as well as light and shade. Arable land is a chance for a landscape designer to impose a style on nature. A theologian may feel closer to God in a garden.

The Bible describes the Garden of Eden as a place of innocence, abundance, beauty, and delight. The sight of a flowering or fruit-laden tree over a garden wall, especially along with the sound of water, retains strong atavistic appeal. This has to do with the desire to overcome the original banishment, replicate the first garden, and return to paradise, or *paradeisos* (the Greek word for garden). A garden also has nature's timeless rhythm, rather than the rapid modern one; despite our quicksilver technology, our hearts beat the same way as at the beginning of time. Working the soil brings me back to my own nature, as I now understand that tending a garden is the same as taking care of myself. My slender sliver of land is less a retreat, or what Simone de Beauvoir called an exile, than a place to repeatedly replenish and ready myself for living outside it.

Even when I am inside, my garden is ever-present behind the house, always drawing my eye outside. It is very different from the bare strip of land I bought twenty years ago. Formerly a forest, it was land for grazing and growing vegetables before it became a place for flowers. The garden and gardener have grown alongside each other over the years, each shaping the other. I eventually knew what to do with the long rectangle of land and how to use its surprising depth. As I learned, I developed more patience, persistence, stamina, and happiness. Every spring offers another chance to undo the damage done by winter and finally get the garden right. I also like knowing that everything was put in the ground by my own hand and seeing how it has added up. The garden has made me aware of the importance of time, of waiting, for growth. Gardening at first felt like a natural pleasure, and then it became a necessary one. While the pleasure began immediately, it took years for the yard to become better defined. Everything about it is fuller now that it is mature. The maple's trunk has thickened, while its crown has risen over the house to its ultimate height of sixty feet.

A grown-up garden is also where the gardener pulls out more than she puts in. After trying almost every perennial that grows in northwestern Connecticut, now, instead of planting something new, I prefer to divide a flourishing flower that is a survivor of both my critical eye and the harsh climate. Not only will it do well elsewhere in my enriched earth, its repetition will be pleasing. *"The immense satisfaction of the garden!"* I wrote during my tenth April in Sharon. *"Even building a better compost bin is good. Shaping environment, making order, working with nature, I suppose."* The rituals of gardening give a rhythm, even rapture, to living, apart from the routines of writing and the ebbs and flows of relationships. Furthermore, by elevating expectations for existence, gardening enhances everyday life. If tending a garden has meant coming under the yoke of the seasons, my capitulation is complete; it is a willed captivity, however, perhaps like any other kind of passion.

Like most gardens, mine is still unfinished. Beyond the boxwood hedges, the backyard remains a largely unplanted place. This is, I tell myself, because of the presence of deer, but the truth is that I like having land to dream on. I have always admired Fred McGourty's idea of a grove of white birches against dark evergreens in back, but I never got around to doing it. Instead, I put a handsome white metal bench that Robert gave me against the privet. The idea of a green garden that takes little work is appealing, as is a yard full of flowering bushes and trees. Maybe I should go ahead and put rows of fruit trees down the length of the yard. I am still unable to rule out a garden-within-a-garden similar to one I sketched in England, with tall junipers anchoring corners, blue statice and iris forming low borders, and pink rosebushes encircling a central pear tree; mine, of course, would need a high fence or hedge to protect it from the foraging deer. Whatever I do, I am glad that my half acre remains open to possibilities for the next twenty years, and I hope that it will at last be as paradisiacal as the garden in my imagination.

acknowledgments

I want to thank the people of Sharon for the many ways they have helped me become a gardener and write this book. Staff members of the Sharon Historical Society and the Hotchkiss Library of Sharon were extremely helpful. A number of other people went out of their way to give me information, notably Betty Grindrod, a founder of the Sharon Garden Club, and Bill Zeller, whose grandfather once owned my house. While I was writing the book, my next-door neighbor, Liz Gall, generously gave me tips of all kinds over the fence while man-of-all-trades Jim Giuseffi good-naturedly helped me outside. Heartfelt thanks go to my friends who were early readers of the manuscript. Judy Mellecker gave me timely and valuable guidance. I am especially grateful to my husband, Robert Kipniss, for his ongoing enthusiasm and encouragement for both my writing and my gardening. Last but not least, thanks go to my longtime agent, Charlotte Sheedy, and to my editors at Random House, Ileene Smith and Robin Rolewicz.

about the author

LAURIE LISLE is a journalist, biographer, essayist, and lecturer who lives in Sharon, Connecticut, and Ardsley-on-Hudson, New York. Raised in Providence, Rhode Island, she comes from a family of New England gardeners.

about the type

This book was set in Granjon, a modern recutting of a typeface produced under the direction of George W. Jones, who based Granjon's design upon the letterforms of Claude Garamond (1480–1561). The name was given to the typeface as a tribute to the typographic designer Robert Granjon.